Gentleman
Junkie

Gentleman Junkie

The Life and Legacy of William S. Burroughs

Graham Caveney

Little, Brown and Company
Boston New York Toronto London

To the memory of my father,
John Caveney,
a man who always hinted at
other possibilities.

First Edition

ISBN 0-316-13725-1
Library of Congress Catalog Card Number 97-76356
10 9 8 7 6 5 4 3 2 1

Designed by Simon Jennings

Published simultaneously in Canada
by Little, Brown & Company (Canada) Limited

Printed in Great Britain
by Butler & Tanner Ltd, Frome, Somerset.

Acknowledgements

Thanks to Tony Peake and David Reynolds who kick-started this project, and to Jo Frankham, Anna Magyar and Duncan Webster who helped keep it afloat.

Thanks also to: my mother, Kathleen Caveney; David Corker, Sally Creelman, James Grauerholz, Julie and David Hesmondalgh, Simon Jennings, Rebecca Kidd, Monica Macdonald, Natasha Marsh, Barry Miles and Edward Taylor.

A special thanks must go to Maggie Maclure and Peter McConnell, without whom I would probably still be locked in the library.

On my saying, 'What have I to do with the sacredness of traditions, if I live wholly from within?' my friend suggested, 'But these impulses may be from below, not from above.' I replied, 'They do not seem to me to be such; but if I am the Devil's child, I will live then from the Devil.' No law can be sacred to me but that of my nature. Good and bad are but names very readily transferable to that or this; the only right is what is after my constitution; the only wrong what is against it.

RALPH WALDO EMERSON, *SELF-RELIANCE*

He who wishes to know the truth about life in its immediacy must scrutinize its estranged form.

THEODOR ADORNO, *MINIMA MORALIA*

Author's Note

In his introduction to the most recent biography of Burroughs, Barry Miles wrote that, 'It is the *idea* of Burroughs that appeals, not the man; the popular Burroughs, the cult icon, reaches them via printed and electronic media. This Burroughs is the man who saw the abyss and came back to report on it.' The achievement of Miles's book is that it reaches out for the man behind the idea, attempting to unearth the individual from the rubble of his iconography.

Five years previous to this, Ted Morgan went on a similar mission. His *Literary Outlaw* is a mammoth bid to cut through the hype and paint a 'warts-and-all' portrait of Burroughs as he really was.

The impetus for this book was born out of an interest in reversing this process – in mapping out how the idea of Burroughs has its own realities, its own narratives; and how the man contains and is contained by their interaction. Rather than rescuing the man from the myth, I intend to speculate on how the one might be located in the other. My project is not to uncover Burroughs's 'authentic personality', but rather to ask why it is that he invites us to wonder whether or not he actually has one.

If there was a truth to Burroughs's life, then what better place to look for it than in the fictions in which it came cloaked? If Burroughs comes across to us as a concept, what is the nature of its fascination? If Burroughs's 'image' is at odds with his 'reality', then what are the dynamics that keep them in dispute; moreover, what is it that is produced by their dialogue?

What is on offer, then, is a chronology of the Burroughs phenomenon, an unpacking of a performance in which the subject is both the spectacle and the spectator.

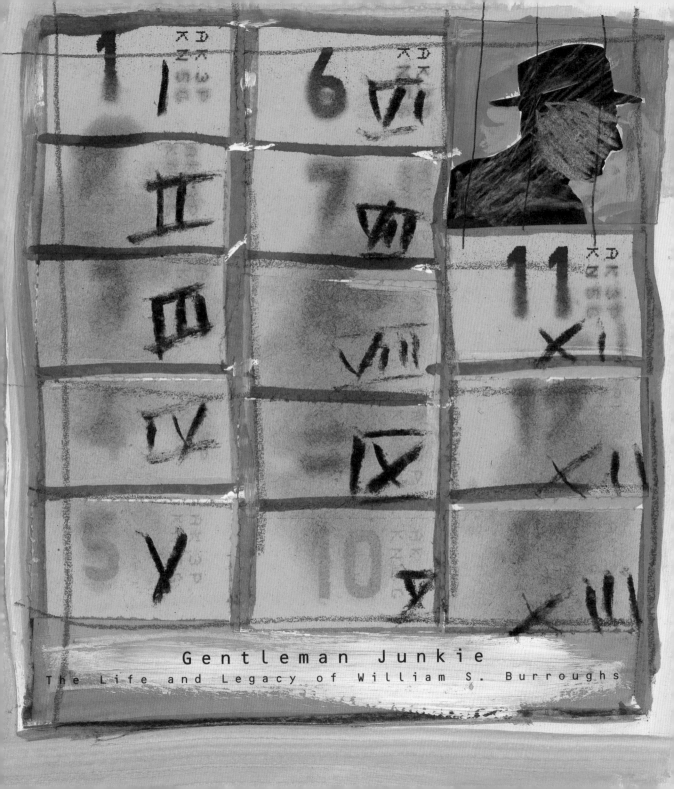

Gentleman Junkie

The Life and Legacy of William S. Burroughs

Introduction

America's literary history has claimed many casualties, its canon being littered by writers who were destroyed by the weight of their own iconography. Victims of their own design, architects of their own destruction – American letters read like the most unforgiving of obituaries. Fitzgerald warned that there were no second acts in American lives – a prophecy he was to fulfil at the age of forty-four, drowning himself in a sea of booze and self-loathing. He was not alone. Hemingway, macho to the end, put a shotgun to his head after six months of sobriety, whilst Faulkner, Kerouac and Chandler were prematurely crushed by their own addictive legacies. The list goes on – Cheever, Carver, Dorothy Parker: American literature is almost a 'who's who' of self-annihilation.

Those who have survived have developed strategies of varying success. Salinger and Pynchon have retreated from the public gaze completely, seeking refuge in paranoid anonymity. The self-styled Gonzo of New Journalism, Hunter S. Thompson, now reads like a caricature of his earlier self, a figure dancing to the tune of someone else's hype. The man who coined the phrase, 'When the going gets weird, the weird turn professional' has proved that when the weird turn professional, their profession becomes predictable.

Yet somehow William Burroughs endures, side-stepping tragic bohemia on the one hand and self-parody on the other. His persona embodies all the ingredients of ruined classicism, yet is defined by none of them. His presence is that of the ghost in the machine – central to its working whilst (n)ever present within it. As Paul Bowles said of him, 'When I got to know him I realized the legend existed in spite of him and not because of him: he didn't give a damn about it.' Maybe it is this indifference that makes him so different. His wilful disregard for his audience gives us a perverse satisfaction, reminding us just how tenuous the contract really is between writer and reader.

At the same time his status exists almost irrespective of his work. His cadaverous features are chiselled on to our collective consciousness, like a face staring out at us from postmodernism's Mount Rushmore. He is a signifier of the terminally hip, a name dropped so frequently that it resurfaces with a (lack of) identity all of its own. He has permeated the very fabric of contemporary culture to such an extent that it is difficult to imagine it without him. Fans of Burroughs become so before they have read him (often without bothering to do so) – the very idea of him is as exciting as his work. Maybe more so. Certainly the titles that have been bestowed on him trip off

Left: Some of
the casualties
of America's
literary history.
(Clockwise from
top left)
Fitzgerald,
Parker, Kerouac,
Hemingway.
Right: Somehow,
William S.
Burroughs
endured...
Photographed here
in Kansas, 1994,
at the age of 80.

the tongue more readily than the titles of his books. The father of the Beats, the godfather of punk, the man who shot his wife, the junkie who reported back, the psychic explorer, the self-pronounced Queer, the literary cosmonaut, the aesthetic outlaw – the epithets bombard us like a newsreel, reducing more mundane ones such as 'The Ticket That Exploded' to mere footnotes.

One of the reasons why Burroughs's books may not be as widely read as his profile suggests is that he himself has not written them. Or not in any conventional manner. Burroughs is an artist who thrives off collaboration, be it anyone from Brion Gysin to Kurt Cobain. He resists our traditional notion of the autonomous author, opting instead for methods of composition which involve the random, the cut-up and the collective. His sources range from newspapers to tape-recordings, thus challenging our assumptions about what it means to be literary. He is a disc jockey of the word, sampling and restructuring the languages that society speaks. Small wonder then that his novels can be reified without being read – his work already exists all around us, his material is constantly affecting us almost by a kind of osmosis. As he was to put it himself, 'The artist makes people aware of what they know, but they don't know that they know.' Burroughs has written no novels, no one has read them, we all lay claim to them. And I'm only half-joking.

If the Burroughs enigma exists in a parallel universe to that of his work, what then is the key to its appeal? Part of the answer must lie in the way that his projection of himself embraces juxtaposition – his ability to hint at contradictions and tease us with their co-existence. His infamous suit and hat suggest an etiquette, with a dirty mind – a bit like meeting your bank manager in a porn shop. His smile lies somewhere between an undertaker's and a card shark's, as though there is an in-joke that you may or may not be in on. The paternalist spills over into the paedophile, the junkie blends easily into the gentleman. There is nothing hidden in Burroughs's image, no secret to be decoded. What is intriguing (and unsettling) about his persona is that no aspect of it takes priority over any other. He does not offer us a choice between his various selves – they are all out in the open, where no one can see them.

In a sense Burroughs's body of work is the candid chiaroscuro of his own status – an amalgam of transparent disguise that patrols the margins of mythology, apocrypha and fable. Like Prospero and Caliban rolled into one, he combines the omnipotent neutrality of the magician with the abject abandon of his assistant. Burroughs may be the only illusionist to saw himself in half.

In strictly literary terms the strength of Burroughs's writing is to be found amongst its many paradoxes. If there is one

American Academy and Institute of Arts and Letters

633 WEST 155 STREET · NEW YORK · N.Y. 10032 *Telephone:* (212) 368-5900

Mr. William S. Burroughs
P.O. Box 147
Lawrence, KS   66044   January 27, 1983

Dear Mr. Burroughs:

I have the honor and pleasure to inform you that you have been elected to the American Academy and Institute of Arts and Letters as a member of the Department of Literature. New members will be invited to attend an informal welcoming dinner on Wednesday, April 6, but formal induction will take place at our public ceremonial to be held on May 18, 1983, at which time you will receive the diploma of the Academy-Institute.

Will you be kind enough to let us know by return mail that you accept election? Please keep this news confidential until it is released to the press some time in February.

Sincerely yours,

Hortense Calisher

Enclosures:
   Brochure
   Membership roster

Hortense Calisher
Secretary of the Institute

20

WILLIAM BURROUGHS COMMUNICATIONS

P.O BOX 147
LAWRENCE, KANSAS 66044
TELEPHONE 913-841-3908

Ms. Hortense Calisher
Secretary of the Institute
American Academy and Institute
    of Arts and Letters
633 West 155th Street
New York   NY   10032

3 February 1983

Dear Ms. Calisher:

Thank you for your letter of January 27th. It is
indeed an honor and a pleasure to accept election
to the American Academy and Institute of Arts and
Letters.

I will plan to be present for the formal induction
in New York on May 18th, and I look forward to taking
part. I may not be able to be present for the dinner
on April 6th, unfortunately, as I live here in Kansas
and, excepting a trip to San Francisco later this
month, will be here all Spring. You may reach me
here with any further information if necessary.

Sincerely yours,

William S. Burroughs

William S. Burroughs

WSB:jg

21

constant running throughout his work then it is surely the fear of control. His novels display an almost psychotic vigilance for imprisoning systems, from drugs and desire through to religion and language. Yet they also capture the allure of control, the masochistic bliss of being enslaved by addiction, sexuality and narrative. He is at once engaged and ethereal – addressing contemporary issues from a standpoint which seems tantalizingly removed from the history of which it speaks. Burroughs may well write of the landscapes of post-war America, yet he refuses to be inscribed within them.

It is this sense of being an exile in his own reality (even a tourist in his own body) that gives Burroughs's work its distinctly European flavour. Whilst Ginsberg's songs of himself echoed the epic poetry of Walt Whitman and Kerouac's road romanticism resurrected the spirit of Huckleberry Finn, Burroughs's ancestors hail from the old world rather than the new. He has frequently acknowledged his debt to Conrad and both his novels and interviews are liberally peppered with Shakespearian allusions.

Similarly his demeanour owes more to the chic criminality of Jean Genet and the grotesque wisdom of De Sade than it does to any image of the Great American Novelist. It is significant that Burroughs should cite Eliot's *The Wasteland* as the first great cut-up – acknowledging his debt to a writer who came to understand his culture via exile. It is now common critical currency to place Burroughs's novels in the tradition of Swiftian satire. Yet one can also detect the influence of Dostoevsky's existential dread, the maniacal eroticism of George Bataille and the insurrectionary vaudeville of Dada.

Burroughs's raiding of a European heritage is reconstructed within a quintessentially American context – yet another illustration of his ability to blur either/or into a composite whole.

Of course the ultimate paradox of the Burroughs mystique is that this most unsaintly of writers has found himself canonized. His induction into the American Academy and Institute of Arts and Letters in 1983 was an occasion replete with ironies. The marginalized and the mainstream converged with mutual unease; the linguistic terrorist whose intent was to Rub Out The Word had finally had it bestowed upon him. And yet this is no return of the prodigal son, nor any simple appropriation by a conspiratorial establishment. Burroughs very much still walks alone, his iconic signature transcribed with an iconoclastic flourish. As in his relationship with the Beats, the yippies or the punks, Burroughs may be in the Academy, but he is certainly not of them. As he was to say later, 'I feel very little empathy with most people. And so when you speak of "we", it would have to be a pretty small "we". Most "we's" you can count me out of.'

Chapter 1

William Seward Burroughs was the product of the entrepreneurial North and the Christ-haunted South an amalgam of the two Americas that had fought each other so bloodily during the Civil War. His paternal grandfather (and namesake) was the embodiment of the self-made Yankee, the man who invented the adding machine and thus became the cornerstone of the Burroughs Corporation. His maternal grandfather, on the other hand, would not have been out of place in a Flannery O'Connor story. A Calvinist preacher who delivered the Word to whoever would listen, he would come to be characterized by Burroughs as 'a circuit-riding Methodist minister'. With a name like James Wideman Lee he could not help but claim blood ties with the South's most famous son, Robert E. Lee, although the connection seems tenuous at best.

With the Bible on one side and the spirit of Capitalism on the other, Burroughs's ancestry is a family therapist's wet dream. His contempt for the platitudes of organized religion, coupled with a maniacal mistrust for the mechanisms of order, could suggest a

career spent striking back against his heritage – a kind of Oedipal struggle at one generation removed. Yet acknowledging the influence of the Burroughs–Lee legacy should not inscribe him within it. A birthright is not the same as a birthmark, and the Burroughs project is clearly much more than a familial squabble.

That said, one of the key figures from Burroughs's past seems to have been his uncle, Ivy Lee. He was blessed with his father's powers of persuasion but decided to use them by working as a turn-of-the-century spin doctor. With his gift for being what Burroughs called 'a master image-maker', Ivy Lee started his career by working as publicity manager to the Rockefellers, and ended it by being investigated by the Committee on Un-American Activities for his covert PR work for the Nazis in 1934. He was an arch-manipulator with an ad-man's scruples, and became known as 'Poison Ivy' via the writings of Upton Sinclair and John Dos Passos.

It is no coincidence that Burroughs was to choose 'Lee' as his pseudonym for his first novel, *Junkie*. Is the choice one which suggests a proud lineage or an ironic curse – William Lee, the descendant who disgraces his family by embracing them? Certainly Burroughs's suspicion of language in all its forms would point towards the idea that his persona as a novelist places him alongside those forces of control against which he is writing. In his *Paris Review* interview with Conrad Knickerbocker, published in 1968, he discusses the links between art and advertising, between high finance and writing:

My uncle Ivy created images for him [Rockefeller]. I fail to understand why people like J. Paul Getty have to come on with such a stuffy, uninteresting image....I'd like to take somebody like Getty and try to find an image for him that would be of some interest. If Getty wants to build an image, why doesn't he hire a first-class writer to write his story?

The incarnation of William Lee is a recognition of how the conman and the artisan are engaged in similar activities – 'After all, they're doing the same sort of thing. They are concerned with the precise manipulation of word and image.' In his uncle Burroughs found a figure through whom he could implicate his project in *Junkie*, a pseudonym that speaks of its own culpability.

If Ivy Lee looms large in Burroughs's work as an emblem of control, the figures of his parents are characterized by a sense of emotional absence. His father, Mortimer, emerges as a man who was both decent and distant – a product of the respectable white-collared Midwest, a class whose public sociability was matched only by its more personal unavailabilty. He worked as a sales rep for the Burroughs Corporation before starting his own plate-glass company in St Louis. In later years he and his wife ran a crafts shop called Cobble Stone Gardens and were affluent enough to give Burroughs an allowance of $200 per month until Burroughs relinquished it in 1960 after making some money from *Naked Lunch*. It was his first son – also called Mortimer – who fulfilled the father's expectations, dutifully following him into the family business before working as a draughtsman for General Electric and staying in St Louis until he retired. Clearly Mortimer Snr was ill-equipped for

Previous page: Uncle Ivy Lee, 1929.
Opposite and following pages: Paternal grandfather and namesake William S. Burroughs, of Burroughs Adding Machine fame, and his Detroit factory, 1904.

dealing with the routes that his second son was to take. William Burroughs was following a script of his own making, and his father did not even begin to try to make sense of it. It outraged, wounded and at times disgusted him, and yet his sense of responsibility meant that he remained loyal to his son despite all the misgivings about his behaviour. The allowance kept coming and William was bailed out by his father after numerous encounters with the police. Mortimer may not have understood his son, but he understood that he *was* his son and acted with the despairing faith of the put-upon patriarch.

Whereas Mortimer's touchstone was containment, Laura Lee veered much more towards neurosis. She disowned her Bible Belt upbringing, though retaining its ersatz mysticism. Reports of her psychic visions range from dreaming of a car crash that had happened the same night to Mortimer Jnr through to gut mistrust of her husband's business partners that turned out to be prophetic. In his interviews with Victor Bockris, Burroughs talks of his mother as being 'enigmatic and complex. Sometimes old and knowing, mostly with a tremulous look of doom and sadness, she suffered from head and back aches, was extremely psychic, and was interested in magic'. Perhaps more significantly he mentions her 'abhorrence of bodily functions', a trait that is picked up on by William Burroughs Jnr in his autobiographical novel, *Kentucky Ham*: 'My grandmother was Laura Lee Burroughs, aristocratic, proud, possessed of great strength and a great disgust for all things pertaining to bodily functions.' Burroughs's fascination for the visceral, for those abject fluids which blur the me and the not-me, could well have their origin in the antiseptic body-horror of his mother. In his fiction the body is often

30

THE HOME OF THE BURROUGHS ADDING AND LISTING MACHINE
ERECTED IN DETROIT IN 1904
A LASTING MONUMENT TO HIS NAME

portrayed as a prison of the self – enslaving us to its appetites and inflicting upon us involuntary desires. If Burroughs took from his father the importance of propriety, this was counterbalanced by his mother's disgusted fascination with the improper – a case of sifting through the bullshit by retaining our own.

Although we may never escape our parents, their stamp is not indelible, and Burroughs does not seem any more (de)formed by them than the rest of us. Indeed, if we compare him to a writer such as Philip Roth, who spent at least a third of his career exorcizing the demons of his childhood, the roles of Laura Lee and Mortimer Burroughs appear almost negligible. Again we are left with the image of Burroughs being *of* but never limited *to* circumstances. His own reticence about his family does not stem from wariness or the desire to conceal. Rather it is the tone of mild disinterest, as though he were talking about acquaintances more than friends, the inhabitants of a world to which he feels no particular debt nor resentment.

THE BIRTHPLACE OF THE BURROUGHS ADDING AND LISTING MACHINE

Burroughs was born in February 1914 – the year that Europe would be thrown into its most savage and bloody conflict to date. The First World War could be read as either the decollation of the civilized world or the culmination of its mercenary logic. For the discontented voices of Modernity it was both. Burroughs was born on the cusp of the Wasteland, an age of anxious values and decimated health. America's involvement in 1917 proved to be its most poisoned chalice. It emerged as an industrially efficient international force, yet one that felt it had achieved economic success at the cost of moral impoverishment. Ezra Pound railed against his 'botched civilization' whom he considered to be a bitch gone rotten in the teeth, whilst Fitzgerald managed to capture the erotic allure of money as well as the desperate vacuity of its purchase. 'Terrible honesty' was how Dorothy Parker described the post-war mood, a phrase which suggests how America was forced to confront the contradictions of benefiting from its lost innocence.

For the family at 4664 Pershing Avenue, St Louis, Missouri, affluence never fully equated itself with security. To an outsider, the three-storey red-brick house on a leafy St Louis street may have seemed the model of suburban comfort. Serviced by a butler, cook and maid, the Burroughs household could hardly be said to have been déclassé. Yet, as the stories of Jimmy Gatz or George Babbitt show, showing some class is different from belonging to one, and it seems that the Burroughses were constantly aware that they had never quite arrived. As Burroughs told Barry Miles, 'The point is we were not rich, and this circumstance alone would have excluded us from any elitist circles. With $200,000 in the bank, we were not accepted by old families with ten, twenty, fifty million....When the WASP elite got together for dinners and lunches and drinks nobody wanted those ratty Burroughses about.' Fitzgerald was keen on reminding us that 'the rich are different'. Burroughs adds that the really rich are really different, and that his family's petit-bourgeois status was as vulgar to those above them as it was enviable to those below. Still, the money from the Burroughs Adding Machine Corporation saw the family through the Great Depression, and the allowance of $200 per month gave Burroughs a privilege that was to be the envy of his Beat friends, particularly Kerouac.

Following pages: John Burroughs School, St Louis; Kells Elvins, Burroughs's contemporary and life-long friend; T.S. Eliot, a Harvard contemporary.

KELLS ELVINS

Born on August 15, 1913, at Elvins, Missouri.
Prepared at John Burroughs School. Home address: Price Road, Clayton, Missouri. In college
three years as undergraduate. Leverett House.
Instrumental Clubs 1932-33.

Field of Concentration: Intended Vocation:
English   Teaching

Kells Elvins

St Louis was a deeply conservative society, unofficially segregated and fond of its traditions and its homespun orthodoxy. It had been the birthplace of T. S. Eliot, who would later write of the humbling impact of growing up so close to the mighty Mississippi. But its sleepy old ways contained a darker, almost Gothic side – as though Poe were to find himself living in a Norman Rockwell painting. Throughout the twenties St Louis still employed a hangman to enforce capital punishment, and it is not inconceivable that Burroughs himself may have witnessed this spectacle of public barbarity. It certainly helps to situate his novels' fixation with hanging as a death which combines sexual *frisson* with collective blood-lust.

THOMAS STEARNS ELIOT
A.M.
Former Charles Eliot Norton Professor of
Poetry

If St Louis thrived on its sense of community (from the Great Books Club to the gallows), Burroughs responded with introspection and withdrawal. His infancy was dominated by obsessive devotion to his nanny, a Welsh woman called Mary Evans. There has been some speculation as to whether their relationship ever became abusive, although the evidence is as foggy as the dreams on which it is based.

At the age of eleven he enrolled in the John Burroughs School (no relation), where he continued to turn his gaze inwards. In an autobiographical sketch entitled 'Meet Me in St Louis Louie', Burroughs wrote of a boy who was 'sadly lacking in social graces and worldly experience. He could not dance, play games, or make light conversation. He was painfully shy....His face was scarred with festering spiritual wounds, and there was no youth in it.' What emerges is a classic portrait of the artist as outsider, a consummate composite of anomic misreadings and wilful alienation.

Two key events rescued Burroughs from his position of adolescent isolation. The first was his friendship with Kells Elvins, a contemporary who seemed to embody all those traits that Burroughs so painfully lacked. He was affable, networked and athletic, at ease with himself and with the girls whom he attracted by the dozen. Their dynamic was homoerotic, sexual on Burroughs's part, social on Elvins's.

Though their relationship never became physical, Burroughs was undoubtedly in the throes of a crush – in love with his friend's heterosexual prowess for providing the necessary obstacle to his own desires. They remained friends right up until Elvins's death in 1962, their paths having continued to cross throughout their time at university as well as in joint excursions to Texas and Tangier.

Burroughs's second significant encounter was with a novel – one of those flukes of reading whereby our inner world becomes crystallized by someone else's vision. Jack Black's *You Can't Win* is a memoir of his life as a petty crook and gambler at the turn of the century in the American West, a seedy low-rent account of the world of hustle. To a thirteen-year-old boy who felt both stifled and ostracized by the mores of the Midwest, Black's book offered a glimpse of a society that not only recognized his marginalization, but actively valued and nurtured it. In *You Can't Win* Burroughs had found his mirror, a rogues' gallery of misfits and immoralists with whom he could identify. Black's outlaws held out the promise of escape – freed by their dispossession, they became the heroes of Burroughs's folklore, a set of role-models in reverse.

In 1929 Burroughs moved to the Los Alamos Ranch School in New Mexico, an establishment founded on rugged (i.e. warped) masculinity and military-style regimentation. The school's director was A. J. Connell, a character so shot through with repressed homosexuality that any caricacature would be flattering. His obsessive regime of outdoor virility and wholesome celibacy makes Baden-Powell sound well adjusted. There was nothing that fresh air and cold showers could not fix, and Burroughs soon found himself subjected to masturbation inspections and that more covert form of sadism known as Physical Education. The boy continued to find refuge in fiction, living off a staple diet of pulp magazines and detective novels. (Of course, this narrative is far from unique. All adolescents worthy of the name experience themselves as angst-ridden outsiders and tend to seek solace in the fantastic truths of art. Not all of them become writers. Most of them become readers. Put another way, Burroughs's childhood was exceptionally normal, or rather normal in that he considered it exceptional.)

Burroughs's own recollections of his school years have a laconic tone of factual disinterest, as though the 'misfit turning to books' script had an inevitable logic. In a piece called 'The Name Is Burroughs' he says of Los Alamos,

I was forced to become a Boy Scout, eat everything on my plate, exercise before breakfast, sleep on a porch in zero weather....We had to stay outdoors, no matter what, all afternoon – they even timed you in the john....What I liked to do was get in my room against the radiator and play records and read the Little Blue Books put out by Haldeman-Julius, free-thinker and benevolent agnostic.

RANCH SCHOOL STUDENT BODY IN 1930

Top Row: George Marston, Hep Blaffer, Dave Harrington, Luke Yule, Denny Dennison, Gardner Carpenter, Flamen Ball, Jay Rice, Stamps Farish.

Second Row: Bernon Woodle, Eddie Hughes, Edgar Marston, Art Wood, Mort Burroughs, Lobo Wood, Clay Pooler.

Third Row: Charlie Hughes, Frank True, Andy Anderson, ?, Pete Lord, ?, ?, Francis Rousseau, Fet Hughes, Mac Wood, ?.

Front Row: Billy Burroughs, Bobby Wheeler, Glenn Wayne, Myron Hall, David Beals, Bobby Marston, Hank Wardwell, Bud Lynch, Hank Dearborn, Walter Edge, Jay Gilchrist, Russ Fawcett, Jeff Farish.

No.	Name	C Camp	Year	No. Years at LA	Grad. of Los Alamos	Rank in Service	Branch of Service
1.	Andrew H. L. Anderson		'34	5	G	Cadet	Army Air Corps
2.	James R. Anderson, Jr.		'38	5	G		Navy Air Corps
3.	Whitney Ashbridge		'19	1	G	Major	Army Engineers
4.	Gordon F. Bell		'35	5	G	Sgt.	Army Anti-Tank Div.
5.	Robert H. Bishop		'33	3			Naval Reserve
6.	John M. Bleakie		'22	3			Naval Reserve
7.	William Burroughs		'31	2		Pvt.	Army
8.	Don T. Chamberlain	C	'21	2		Major	Army Medical Corps
9.	James A. Chapin		'35	3		Ensign	Naval Intelligence

L·A·R·S

Previous pages: (left) Burroughs at Los Alamos Ranch School, 1930; (right) school Director A. J. Connell, 1934. This page: Los Alamos Ranch School and environs; the 1930 student body; Los Alamos Alumni Bulletin, summer 1942 – service record of ex-students includes Burroughs as army private.

The school's emphasis on sport did have its upside in that it allowed Burroughs to pursue his interest in shooting. This was the one pastime he had engaged in with his father, and one that he maintained as an on-and-off fixture to the end of his life.

It was also during his time at the Ranch School that Burroughs engaged in his first experiment with drugs – an encounter with some store-bought chloral hydrate that resulted in him being carried home by the school nurse. The ever-myopic Connell wrote a stern letter to his parents that also reassured them: 'I believe he realizes now that it was a fool thing to do and I doubt if he will try anything like it again.' Connell will hardly be remembered as a visionary, and several more pranks on Burroughs's part, coupled with another adolescent crush, resulted in him leaving Los Alamos under a cloud of hushed-up insolence and homosexual rumour.

His failure to graduate necessitated a brief stint at a private tuition college in St Louis before he could be accepted at Harvard. The latter was a choice that owed more to parental expectation than to Burroughs's own motivation.

He arrived in Cambridge, Mass. in 1932, a year that saw America sink to the depths of the Depression, with 25 million unemployed and a deficit that today would make most Third World countries feel that they had never had it so good. Artists responded to the Depression with either deep-seated reaction or calls for radical mobilization. This was the decade that spawned not only the agit-prop of Odets, tragic naturalism of Steinbeck and the docu-dramatic realism of Dos Passos, but also the right-wing whimsy of *Gone with the Wind* and the agrarian nostalgia of the South's New Critics.

Harvard, like most academic institutions, encompassed both political stances, attracting the fashionable left who sought to revolutionize intellectualism as well as the rarefied right who battled to uphold it. The English department, to which Burroughs belonged, contained card-carrying Communists such as F. O. Matthiessen, who taught alongside diehard aesthetes such as George L. Kittredge. Such pluralism did not force Burroughs into choosing sides so much as confirm him in his belief that he should avoid the debate altogether. Perhaps more significant was the impact of T. S. Eliot, who delivered the poetry lectures during his first year at Harvard. Burroughs never had any direct contact with Eliot, although the Great Modernist's contempt for the excesses of Romanticism and his call for art both to absorb tradition and then to Make It New resonates throughout Burroughs's work.

His year book at Harvard is quite literally a blank, with nothing beneath his picture but his name and address. There were neither clubs nor fraternities, no sports and few friends. Burroughs's undergraduate years appear to have been spent cultivating the art of invisibility, casting himself as a fugitive from an establishment of which he was a part. Recalling these years later, he dismissed them with an adamant disdain: 'I didn't like Harvard at all, I don't like Boston, I didn't like Cambridge. I didn't like the whole atmosphere....I was just a completely beat down person with no idea of who he was or what he was. And I'd rather not think about it ever since then.' The only debt that Burroughs feels he owes Harvard is that it taught him 'how to use a library....I'm not talking about research, I'm talking about reading; the English classics and the French.'

This particular part of his past really is a foreign country. They did things differently there, and so, it seems, did Burroughs.

Burroughs sent this for use in
the 25th anniversary album
it was not used. His 1936
class photo was used
instead.

WILLIAM SEWARD BURROUGHS
    Born on February 5, 1914, in St. Louis,
Missouri. Home address: Box 1017, Price Road,
Clayton, Missouri. In college four years. Claverly.
Field of Concentration:
English

Pg 108   1936 Harvard Class Album

ROBERT THOMPSON BROWN, Jr.

Born on September 7, 1915, in Jamaica, New York. Prepared at St. Paul's. Home address: 164-27 Highland Avenue, Jamaica, New York. In college four years. Leverett House.

Field of Concentration: Intended Vocation:
Government   Business

ALAN BURNHAM

Born on February 10, 1913, in Englewood, New Jersey. Prepared at Fountain Valley. Home address: Orchard Way, Berwyn, Pennsylvania. In college four years. Dunster House.

Field of Concentration: Intended Vocation:
Fine Arts   Architecture

THORNTON BROWN

Born on November 24, 1913, in Boston. Prepared at Milton Academy. Home address: 341 Highland Street, Milton, Massachusetts. In college four years. Eliot House. Freshman year: Second Football; Hockey. Junior Varsity Football (3-4); Junior Varsity Hockey (2); Hockey Team (3, 4). Instrumental Clubs. Hasty Pudding Theatricals (2). Hasty Pudding-Institute of 1770: Varsity Club; D. U. Club.

Field of Concentration: Intended Vocation:
Bio-Chemical Sciences   Medicine

DANIEL HUDSON BURNHAM, Jr.

Born on July 2, 1914, in Evanston, Illinois. Prepared at Middlesex School. Home address: 83 Cedar Street, Chicago. In college four years. Adams House. Speakers Club.

Field of Concentration: Intended Vocation:
Economics   Banking

JOHN WINSLOW BRYANT

Born on May 8, 1914, in Milton, Massachusetts. Prepared at Milton Academy. Home address: 149 Randolph Avenue, Milton, Massachusetts. In college four years. 52 Mt. Auburn Street. Freshman year: Intramural Football, Manager, Track, Manager (4). Hasty Pudding-Institute of 1770: D. U. Club.

Field of Concentration: Intended Vocation:
English   Law

DONALD GARDNER BURNS

Born on July 5, 1914, in Boston. Prepared at New Preparatory. Home address: 83 Marlboro Street, Boston. In college two and one-quarter years.

Field of Concentration:
Biology

HENRY STURGES BULLARD

Born on October 3, 1914, in New York City. Prepared at Kent. Home address: Manhasset, Long Island, New York. In college four years. Eliot House.

Field of Concentration: Intended Vocation:
Physics   Business

ROY EMERSON BURNS

Born on February 15, 1915, in Boston. Prepared at Walpole High School. Home address: 20 Gould Avenue, East Walpole, Massachusetts. In college four years. Adams House.

Field of Concentration: Intended Vocation:
Biology   Medicine

EDWARD JOSEPH BURKE

Born on March 22, 1914, in Boston. Prepared at Browne and Nichols. Home address: 26 Allen Street, Boston. In college four years. Living at home. Glee Club (2-4).

Field of Concentration: Intended Vocation:
English   Business

WILLIAM SEWARD BURROUGHS

Born on February 5, 1914, in St. Louis, Missouri. Home address: Box 1017, Price Road, Clayton, Missouri. In college four years. Claverly.

Field of Concentration:
English

43

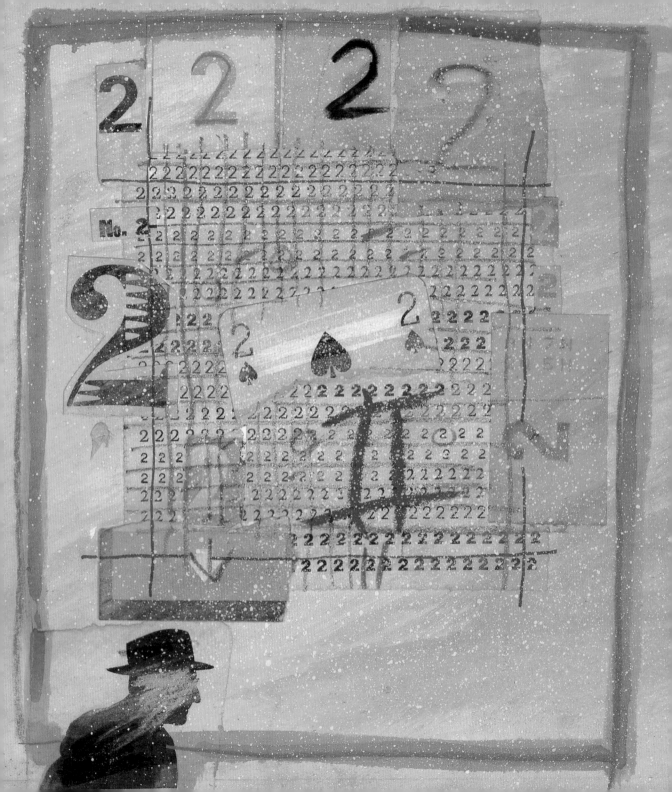

Chapter 2

On his graduation from Harvard in June 1936 Burroughs embarked upon the obligatory tour of Europe – a kind of informal finishing-school for the educated upper class. With one of his few university friends, Bob Miller, he travelled from Paris to Vienna, finding in these cities' Old World decadence the promise of high intellectualism and low sexual morals. Café society and the gay sub-culture were not the mutual exclusives they had been in America, and an interest in boys seemed almost a prerequisite for any self-respecting artisan.

Ironically, it was precisely this alternative atmosphere that led to Burroughs embarking on a project that anywhere else would have been anathema to him. On a visit to Dubrovnik in Yugoslavia he was introduced to a woman called Ilse Klapper, an Austrian Jew who was fleeing from the Nazis and supporting herself by teaching English. At the age of thirty-five, and with one marriage behind her, Ilse embodied for Burroughs the kind of worldly sagacity that he had failed to find at Harvard. She was widely connected, rich in anecdotes, and her exiled status struck a chord with his own sense of always belonging elsewhere. Ilse's visa was due to expire in 1937 and the threat of a Nazi invasion of the Balkans seemed imminent. Marriage to an American would quite literally save her life, and in July 1937, using the ring from her previous marriage, in a small church in Athens

Burroughs and Ilse became man and wife. It was a marriage in name only, but it allowed Ilse to move to New York where she stayed until after the war, later settling in Zurich.

Burroughs has often been accused of rampant misogyny, and not without good reason, yet this one altruistic episode illustrates just how deeply embedded was his sense of doing the right thing. Whilst often projecting himself as the ultimate immoralist – a man for whom right and wrong are selfish expedients – there also exists the old-style gent, a man who cannot stop himself from standing up when a woman enters the room and whose outlaw behaviour is simply another form of etiquette. In his own terminology his marriage to Ilse was the act of a Johnson, a term that he defines in *The Adding Machine*:

In this world of shabby rooming houses, furtive gray figures in dark suits, hop joints and chill parlors the Johnson family took shape as a code of conduct. To say someone is a Johnson means he keeps his word and honors his obligations. He's a good man to do business with and a good man to have on your team. He is not a malicious, snooping, interfering, self-righteous, trouble-making person....A Johnson minds his own business. But he will give help when help is needed.

In 1936 Burroughs embarked upon the obligatory tour of Europe. He travelled from Paris to Vienna, finding in these cities Old World decadence, the promise of high intellectualism and low sexual morals, café society and gay sub-culture.

Burroughs returned from Europe to a St Louis that held few options. His parents had disapproved of his marriage, and his friend Kells Elvins had returned to Harvard to take a postgraduate course in psychology. It was the influence of Elvins that eventually persuaded him to pursue the same route, although Burroughs's subject was to be anthropology.

JOHNSON

EARNS $100 A WEEK...
...and he's heading for success

MR. B, at $100 a week, is already ear-marked for success. For he knows where he stands today... what's more, he knows where he is going tomorrow. With an eye to the future he has drawn his own *Analagraph* plan... a plan that provides amply for his family's tomorrow... yet permits comfortable living today.

Harvard was still as unappealing in 1938 as it had been when he left it – departmental politics and faculty lunches holding more sway than the ideas they were there to encourage. That said, Burroughs did not feel as ostracized as he had done previously, especially since he was sharing a house with Elvins on a back street in Cambridge. It was here that he began experimenting with writing, his first piece being a satire written jointly with Elvins about the sinking of the *Titanic*. He describes the process in 'The Name Is Burroughs':

'To say someone is a Johnson means he keeps his word and honors his obligations. He's a good man to do business with and a good man to have on your team.'

On a screened porch we started work on a story called 'Twilight's Last Gleamings' which was later used almost verbatim in *Nova Express*....We acted out every scene and often got on laughing jags. I hadn't laughed like that since my first tea-high at eighteen when I rolled around the floor and pissed all over myself. I remember the rejection note from *Esquire*: 'Too screwy and not effectively so for us.'

As in his later work with Ginsberg and Gysin, collaboration was the key to Burroughs's creative flow. It is ironic that a figure who seems to stand so much alone has always drawn on the influences of those around him.

The idea of an 'acting out', or what he would later term 'the routine', also sets the tone for his later work, suggesting how the power of a piece resides in its drama – the way in which language can be made to perform the dark humour that it describes. It is no coincidence that Burroughs is consumed as often on tape as he is on the page, or that his readings evoke the kind of rhythmic danger of Lenny Bruce rather than the high solemnity of a literary function. Burroughs's work suggests its own delivery, reflecting and mimicking the mode of its composition.

'Twilight's Last Gleamings' also featured the first appearance of Dr Benway – a character who would most famously dominate *The Naked Lunch*. In both the way it was written and the themes it addressed, this piece could be described as the first produced by the Burroughs-to-be.

When Elvins landed a job as a prison psychologist in Texas, Burroughs could see no reason for staying in Cambridge and returned to St Louis. He had already encountered the work of the semantician Alfred Korzybski, particularly his book *Science and Sanity*, and on hearing that he was running a course on this subject in Chicago Burroughs quickly enrolled. Korzybski was a master polemicist whose project was to dismantle Aristotelian logic and wage war on binary systems of thought. If the choice was always either/or, he argued, then language acted contrary to our experience, which told us that issues tended to be both/and. Words thus referred only to themselves and not to the reality they claimed to describe.

His theory is in many ways the forerunner of contemporary deconstruction, but in the context of the late 1930s it had an impact that resounded with a great deal more urgency. For a period whose buzz-words were 'appeasement', 'National Socialism' and 'peace in our time', it is easy to see how such signifiers were being used as a smokescreen for the more terrifying signifier of a Nazi dictatorship. Clearly language was being used not to engage with history, but rather to deny it. Korzybski is a thinker to whom Burroughs constantly refers in interviews and essays, and it is only a small step to see how his view of language as essentially duplicitous makes sense of why Burroughs would later be attracted to assaulting it via the cut-up. As he was to later explain,

> My general theory…has been that the Word is literally a
> virus, and that it has not been recognized as such because it

has achieved a state of relatively stable symbiosis with its human host....The Word clearly bears the single identifying feature of a virus: it is an organism with no internal function other than to replicate itself.

If 'Twilight's Last Gleamings' was the prototype for Burroughs the novelist, his time spent studying under Korzybski can be read as the origin of his ongoing war against the word.

Profound though its effect might have been, a theory of general semantics did not solve the immediate problem of what Burroughs was to do next. An application to join the Navy was turned down on physical grounds and an attempt to join the OSS (later to be the CIA) was stillborn when it transpired that the interview for the job would be conducted by his former house master at Harvard. Burroughs spent most of 1939–41 working as a delivery boy for his parents' gift shop, and breaking the monotony by making regular visits to friends in New York.

Having failed to enlist in the military before America entered the war, after the bombing of Pearl Harbor the stakes were reversed and Burroughs ended up being drafted. It was his mother who came to the rescue, using her connection with a Washington-based psychiatrist to have her son diagnosed as mentally unsuitable for military service. Burroughs's penance was that he would have to attend a treatment centre outside Washington called Chestnut Lodge, a psych-evaluation unit where he eventually spent six months.

The only significant benefit of his treatment at the Lodge was his friendship with Ray Masterson, a soldier who was pulling a similar scam and who convinced Burroughs of the excitement and employment to be had in his native Chicago. On his discharge in the summer of 1942, Burroughs took Masterson's advice and, with his $200 allowance, went to find work in the Windy City.

William Burroughs recording his own work, at Red House Recording Studio   Sept. 1992

Above: Burroughs recording
his own work at the Red House
Studio in Lawrence, Kansas,
September 1992. The idea of
an acting out, or what he would
later term the routine,
suggests how the power of a
piece resides in its drama —
the way in which language can
be made to perform the dark
humour that it describes.
Burroughs is consumed as often
on tape as he is on the page.
Right: Movie still from *Towers
Open Fire*.

53

Chapter 3

The huge number of men away fighting in the war meant that work was easy to come by, and Burroughs soon landed a job as a bugman for A. J Cohen, Exterminators. His employment gained him access to Chicago's seedier sides, the roach-infested apartments and run-down rooming houses that he had first encountered in the writing of Jack Black. It was in Chicago that Burroughs's fascination with lower-than-life characters first crystallized. His role as exterminator is the first real incarnation of Burroughs the assassin, a man thriving on infestation even as he eradicates it. Insects provide a potent metaphor for his work - symbols of invasion, Kafkaesque pastiches that suggest the proximity of humanity to disease. Burroughs would later mobilize this myth directly in his book *Exterminator!*, a collection of short stories, not to mention the addiction-as-metamorphosis image that dominates *The Naked Lunch*.

Burroughs was joined in Chicago by two friends from St Louis, Lucien Carr and David Kammerer. Kammerer was a homosexual who had shared Burroughs's rejection of St Louis stuffiness, while Carr was a young eccentric student with whom Kammerer was obsessed. Wild times were the norm, and eventually Burroughs was

ejected from his lodgings when his landlady discovered that the three of them had been tearing up the *en suite* Bible and pissing out of the window. Carr was as irritated as he was flattered by Kammerer's attentions and decided to get away from him by enrolling at Columbia University in New York. Kammerer ignored the hint and followed him. Burroughs, who had stuck at his job for eight months and was becoming bored, and who had now also been made homeless, had no further reason to stay in Chicago. He decided to join the dysfunctional couple and explore the allure of New York.

Burroughs landed a job as a bugman. His role as exterminator is the first real incarnation of a man thriving on infestation. Insects provided a potent metaphor for his future work — particularly *Exterminator!*, a collection of short stories, and *The Naked Lunch*.

Whilst Carr immersed himself in the academic excitement of Columbia, Burroughs and Kammerer took up residence in Greenwich Village – the former at 69 Bedford Village Street, the latter around the corner on Morton Street. Manhattan had already established itself as the home of Modernism in the twenties, and this legacy continued through the forties with the arrival of the artistic avant-garde – abstract expressionists, jazz musicians, photographers and aspiring writers. Burroughs and Kammerer had found their spiritual home, a bohemia in which artistry and criminality were seamlessly interwoven. They became regular patrons of the San Remo Bar and the Minetta Tavern – places that had already begun to lend the outlaw an aesthetic dimension, and would later become the hallowed haunts of beatnik folklore.

Carr lived a hundred blocks away and remained in regular contact. On one of these visits to Burroughs he brought with him a recent acquaintance from Columbia – a nervous, bespectacled, seventeen-year-old Jewish boy from New Jersey. His name was Allen Ginsberg. The poet recalls being immediately impressed by

David Eames Kammerer

STUDENT IS SILENT ON SLAYING FRIEND

Held Without Bail After He Listens Lackadaisically to Charge in Stabbing Case

Clasping a copy of "A Vision," a philosophic work by W. B. Yeats, under one arm, Lucien Carr, 19-year-old Columbia sophomore, listened lackadaisically to the proceeding as he was arraigned yesterday morning before Magistrate Anna M. Kross in Homicide Court. He was held without bail for a hearing on Aug. 29.

The pale, slender youth showed little interest as Detective James O'Brien presented a short affidavit charging him with homicide for having fatally stabbed on Monday David Kammerer, 33-year-old former instructor at Washington University, St. Louis, with whom he had been friendly. His attorney, Vincent J. Malone, told the court that the defendant had nothing to say.

Court Asks Psychiatric Test

Magistrate Kross asked Mr. Malone whether he had any objection to having Carr sent to Bellevue Hospital for psychiatric observation at this time. Mr. Malone replied that he did object and

HELD FOR HOMICIDE

Lucien Carr as he was arraigned yesterday.   The New York Times

Kammerer's Parents Prominent

Special to THE NEW YORK TIMES.

ST. LOUIS, Aug. 16—David Kammerer was the son of socially prominent Mr. and Mrs. Alfred L. Kammerer of Clayton, Mo., a suburb of St. Louis. His father is a consulting engineer. The son was graduated from John Burroughs School here in 1929 and from Washington University in 1933.

After some teaching experience

STUDENT MURDERS FRIEND, SINKS BODY

Columbia Student Kills Friend And Sinks Body in Hudson River

LUCIEN AND DAVID

day. Appearing greatly concerned at the high bail, he pleaded with Judge Sullivan to reduce it to a point that his parents, who live

58

Burroughs, a figure who seemed to him full of wisdom and wide reading. 'I had always respected him as elder & wiser than myself, and in first years' acquaintance was amazed that he treated me with respect at all,' he was to write later. Carr and Ginsberg provided a gateway through which Burroughs gained access to the Columbia crowd, a circle that most significantly included Jack Kerouac and his girlfriend Edie Parker.

As the friendship between Burroughs, Ginsberg and Kerouac solidified, that between Carr and Kammerer was rapidly deteriorating. Carr's attachment to his girlfriend in Chicago – a half-French student named Celine Young – served only to inflame Kammerer's infatuation further. On a booze-fuelled night in August 1944 Kammerer threatened to kill both Carr and himself if they could not be together. A fight ensued, in the course of which Carr pulled a knife and stabbed the older man twice through the heart. He dumped the body in the Hudson before going to Burroughs's apartment to tell him what had happened. Burroughs advised him to get a lawyer and to claim self-defence. It took two days of soul-searching and Dutch courage in the bars around the Village before Carr found the nerve to turn himself in. He eventually plea-bargained down to manslaughter and served two years at the Elmira Reformatory. Burroughs and Kerouac were both charged for their failure to report a homicide, then released.

> Burroughs was joined in Chicago by two friends from St Louis, Lucien Carr and David Kammerer. On a booze-fuelled night in August 1944, Carr pulled a knife and stabbed Kammerer twice through the heart.

Far from disabusing them of their libertarian lifestyles, the Kammerer killing seemed to confirm the group's belief that their world-view was well grounded. The homosexual angle of the murder may have helped Carr's case, but it also illustrated an in-built judicial

HERBERT HUNCKE

TIMES SQ.
AT 42ND ST.

The Magic That Changes Moods!

Danceteria
30 W 21st NYC 10010 TEL 212-620-0515
...open 7 nights...

EMPIRE STATE OBSERVATORIES
SOUVENIR RECEIPT
OF A VISIT TO THE
TOP OF THE
WORLD'S
TALLEST BUILDING
847110

60

prejudice against sexual freedom. Furthermore, the fact that Burroughs and Kerouac had been arrested for not informing on their friend showed just how wide the gap was between the Citizens and the Johnsons. Twenty years later Bob Dylan would write: 'To live outside the law you must be honest' – a lesson that Burroughs and his friends had learned the hard way.

A more positive outcome of Kammerer's murder was that it inspired Burroughs to start writing again, this time a collaboration with Kerouac entitled 'And the Hippos Were Boiled in Their Tanks'. But the project never really got into its stride. Burroughs remained taciturn about Kerouac's contributions, whilst he felt himself too close to the incident to afford it the gravity it deserved. It was rejected by publishers, and Burroughs later agreed with their decision: 'People ask me if I ever intend to publish it and I say, no, it isn't very good, it isn't worth publishing.'

As a counterpoise to the student-led Columbia group Burroughs cultivated contacts amongst the hustlers of Times Square. He began to act as a go-between for stolen goods, illegal handguns and morphine syrettes. One of the key players in this twilight world of petty thievery was Herbert Huncke, a small-time crook and addict who had been living off his unscrupulous wits from the age of twelve. Huncke the Junkie was the personification of a type that Norman Mailer would later term 'The White Negro' – the hipster whose only values stem from 'the rebellious imperatives of the self'. Kerouac described him as 'weary, indifferent, yet somehow astonished too, aware of everything. He had the look of a man who is sincerely miserable in the world.' For

ARTHUR RIMBAUD

JACK 1944

ALLEN PARIS 1956

JACK

BILL

ALLEN

HAL CHASE

62

1944

Burroughs he was the Jack Black world incarnate and soon became his street mentor, guiding him through the lower depths of conmanship.

Burroughs moved fluently between the literary uptown of Columbia and the downtown villainy of 42nd Street until he eventually became the magnet that drew the two worlds together. Burroughs introduced Ginsberg to Huncke, who in return introduced Ginsberg to benzedrine. The traffic was flowing both ways – Huncke gave the writers an entrée into the streets, while they provided him with a smokescreen behind which he could hide what he was actually doing on the streets. Given the circumstances it was almost inevitable that Burroughs would experiment with drugs, and Huncke eagerly taught him how to persuade doctors to write morphine prescriptions. By 1944 Burroughs had his first smack habit.

Allen Ginsberg, a nervous, bespectacled, seventeen-year-old Jewish boy. Through Ginsberg Burroughs gained access to the Columbia crowd, a circle that most significantly included Jack Kerouac and Joan Vollmer.

As the two sides of his life coalesced, a further figure was to enter Burroughs's life and bring it to a state of chaotic cohesion. Joan Vollmer was a student of journalism at Columbia, who was bringing up a daughter from a recently defunct marriage when she moved into an apartment on 115th Street with Edie Parker and Kerouac. Her room-mates enlisted Ginsberg's help to bring her and Burroughs together. 'Jack and I decided that Joan and Bill would make a great couple,' recalls Ginsberg. 'They were a match for each other, fit for each other, equally tuned and equally witty and funny and intelligent and equally well read, equally refined.' They were also equally interested in drug-taking, with Joan consuming benzedrine at an impressive rate – so

out of this century

peggy guggenheim

Manhattan had already established itself as the home of Modernism in the twenties, and this legacy continued through the forties with the arrival of the artistic avant-garde. Burroughs and Kammerer became regular patrons of the San Remo Bar and the Minetta Tavern places that would later become the hallowed haunts of beatnik folklore.

65

20¢ EXTRA FARE BELOW THIS POINT

JAMAICA BAY

Joan Vollmer was a student of journalism at Columbia, who was bringing up a daughter from a recently defunct marriage. 'Jack and I decided that Joan and Bill would make a great couple,' recalled Ginsberg. Joan was aware of Burroughs's homosexuality but saw no conflict of interest, jokingly complimenting him that he made love like a pimp.

much so that she was prone to fits of psychosis, aural hallucinations and paranoia. Yet she appeared composed around her new lover, who shared her interest in Mayan magic and appreciated her acerbic sense of humour. Joan was aware of Burroughs's homosexuality but saw no conflict of interest, jokingly complimenting him that he made love like a pimp.

In the summer of 1945 Burroughs moved into Joan's apartment and, when Edie Parker left after she and Kerouac split up, Ginsberg settled there too. It is from this point that the nucleus of a Beat family began to take shape: Ginsberg, Kerouac, Burroughs and Joan all living under the same roof, an alternative household sharing drugs, books, sex and ideas. The group would often play out various psycho-dramas, role-playing routines in which each member would assume the guise of some unlikely character and interact with other characters in an extemporaneous routine. A nineteenth-century lesbian governess, a Hungarian psycho-analyst, a cracker-barrel Southern sheriff – all regular personae for their own entertainment.

Not that this scene was necessarily all fun and games. Joan was relying heavily on nasal inhalers to get her benzedrine rush and was becoming more and more prone to paranoia. She began imagining that some of her neighbours were accusing her of running a brothel, whilst others were trying to murder each other. Hysteria and hallucinations became as commonplace as discussions about poetry, and with Kerouac hitting the bottle and Burroughs on the needle, the whole place was deteriorating into dysfunction and dependence. When the place was eventually busted for narcotics in April 1946 there was a sense of tragic inevitability about the raid. Burroughs, who had been forging prescriptions, was given a four-month suspended sentence and released into the custody of his father. Huncke began renting his now vacant room until he himself was arrested for handling stolen goods and wound up in the Bronx County Jail.

In Burroughs's absence Joan's condition became acute, her speed-use culminating in her having to be admitted to Bellevue psychiatric hospital for a ten-day detox. Given that they were about to be evicted anyway for non-payment of rent, Ginsberg abandoned the apartment and wrote to Burroughs informing him of Joan's illness. Burroughs behaved like a Johnson, returning to New York and renting a hotel room for himself and Joan. New York, it seemed, was devouring them and so, whilst Joan rested in their hotel in Times Square, Burroughs began devising ways for them to get out unscathed.

Chapter 4

During the time spent with his parents
Burroughs had hitched up with his old friend Kells
Elvins, who was planning to start a cotton and citrus
business with some land he had bought in Pharr, Texas.
Burroughs's parents approved of the scheme and bought
him 50 acres, urging him to go with Elvins. Joan had
become pregnant in the course of her recovery, and a
ranch in Texas held out the glimmer of a brand-new
start. After the urban burn-out of New York, Burroughs
and Joan entertained a fantasy of rustic retreat, their
very own Walden where they could live like good
country people. In January 1947 they moved to New
Waverley, near Houston.

But their image of a rural idyll was stillborn from
the start. The couple invited Huncke to join them, and
he was soon making trips to Houston to buy inhalers for
Joan, morphine for Burroughs and marijuana seeds as a crop. The
Waltons they weren't, and drug use became the most convenient way
of killing the time. Their house had no running water or electricity,
and Burroughs's description of the ranch to Ginsberg is anything but
pastoral: 'It is practically Summer down here, and king size scorpions,
Tarantulas, Ticks, chiggers and mosquitos are emerging in droves. I
killed 10 scorpions yesterday. The house is overrun with huge rats as
big as possums....I am contemplating the purchase of a ferret.'

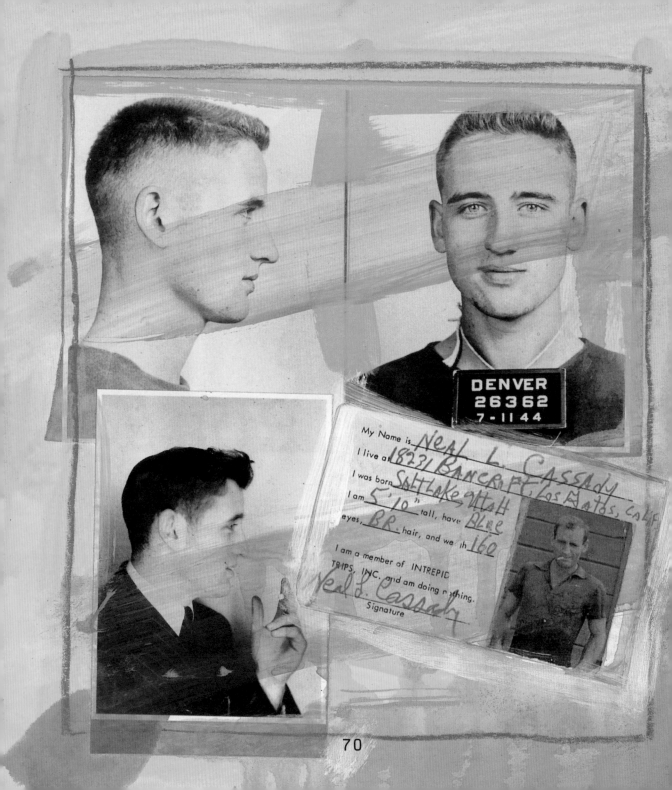

His laconic wit could not disguise the fact that their time in Texas was tedious and bleak. On 21 July Joan went into labour and gave birth to William Burroughs III, a child who was born addicted to speed and spent his first few weeks in the world going through an involuntary detox. In fact Joan had to bottle-feed her baby as her own breast milk was laced with amphetamines.

Ginsberg brought his new love, Neal Cassady, down for a visit, to find a household that was as singularly strung-out as the one he had shared with them in New York. Even worse, his attempt to seduce Cassady failed – a failure that he conveniently blamed on Burroughs's domestic shambles. He stayed only a few days before leaving for West Africa.

Neither was the venture profitable. When Cassady, Huncke and Burroughs drove the 2000 miles back to New York with their pot crop, they found a barren market. Eventually they cut their losses and sold the whole stash for $100 wholesale.

If further proof were needed that it was time to leave Texas, it came when Burroughs was arrested for having drunken sex with Joan in his car. A fine of $173, the loss of his licence and the attention of the police were enough to convince him. Joan and Burroughs sold the farm and tried another new start, this time at 509 Wagner Street in Algiers, Louisianna.

If Texas had been perceived as a haven from drugs, New Orleans was sought out as their heaven. The Big Easy lived up to its name, abundant in junk connections and dope peddlers. The appeal of New Orleans was also its downfall, as Joan's speed habit and Burroughs's own junk sickness gradually brought them to a state of virtual paralysis. Eventually their house was raided and the police uncovered stashes of heroin, marijuana and a collection of firearms. 'If convicted,' Burroughs wrote to Ginsberg, 'I am subject to 2–5 years in Angola [one of the meanest state penitentiaries in the country] which is definitely not a Country Club.' Fortunately his lawyer proved that the search had been illegal, but he

Ginsberg brought his new love, Neal Cassady (left), down for a visit.

also advised Burroughs that it would be politic to leave the country. Late in 1949 Burroughs took Joan and the children and moved to Mexico City.

The period stretching from New York to New Orleans provided the raw material for his first novel, *Junkie*, although it was not until his arrival in Mexico that he began to conceive of writing it. He had taken a course at Mexico City College in Mayan anthropology when Kells Elvins came to visit and suggested that he write about his experiences with heroin. On 1 May 1950 he wrote to Ginsberg, 'I have been working on a novel about junk. It is about finished now. May realize a few $, but I doubt if anyone will publish it, owing to the criticism of the Nar. [cotics] dept. it contains.' By the end of that year, as he and his family were settling into their new home on 37 Cerrada de Medellin, the first draft of the book was complete.

As the manuscript gathered dust, Burroughs continued his on-and-off courtship of junk, and Joan's taste for inhalers increased. Booze had also become a key factor in their lifestyle. Whenever Burroughs kicked heroin he would use alcohol as a substitute, drinking straight tequila for eight-hour stretches. At one point he developed uremia and was advised by his doctor to return to morphine. For Joan, drink and speed perversely complemented each other – the booze took the edge off her speed-paranoia, and the speed allowed her to consume more booze.

'I killed 10 scorpions yesterday. The house is overrun with huge rats as big as possums.'

It was against this background of self-destructive co-dependence that the event that would change Burroughs's life for ever took place. On 6 September 1951 he and Joan decided to sell one of his handguns via their friend John Healy. They had been drinking all afternoon before arriving at Healy's apartment at 6 p.m. When the buyer failed to show up, the couple continued to hit the bottle. Joan had been taunting Burroughs all day, daring him to prove his marksmanship. 'I began throwing down one drink after the other,' said Burroughs. 'I was very drunk. I suddenly said, "It's time for our William Tell act. Put a glass on your head."' With the carefree abandon of a hardened drinker, Joan laughingly agreed, although it was the first time they had played the game. She balanced a six-ounce water glass on her head, and Burroughs fired a bullet through her temple. The pronouncement of death at the Red Cross Hospital was a formality.

Much speculation has been given to the killing. Was Joan suicidal, or acting out the nihilistic bravado of an alcoholic? Was Burroughs homicidal and using the game as a cover for murder? There was certainly nothing premeditated about the event, and the most plausible explanation is simply that Joan's death was an accident brought about by drunken abandon. The most tragic irony of the episode is that Joan's death forced Burroughs into taking himself seriously as a writer. As he was to comment later,

I am forced to the appalling conclusion that I would never have become a writer but for Joan's death, and to a realization of the extent to which this event has motivated and formulated my writing. I live with the constant threat of possession, and a constant need to escape from possession, from Control. So the death of Joan brought me in contact with the invader, the Ugly Spirit and manoeuvered me into a lifelong struggle, in which I have had no choice except to write my way out.

Joan's ghost remained with Burroughs to the end and it's not difficult to read his shotgun paintings (in which a can of paint is placed in front of a canvas and exploded by rifle or handgun) as his attempt to exorcize her – a case of art imitating death.

146 Colt's

Revolver, or blued or stock finished, l: length, : 6 shot, : 4½ or 6 in. barrels, 28 No. 47108 cartridges.

CARTRIDGES

Chapter 5

Released on bail after thirteen days, Burroughs had to await the sentencing that was set for a year later (he was eventually charged with *imprudencia criminal*). The volatility of the Mexican legal system made him feel uneasy – corruption, after all, could cut both ways. His suspicions were confirmed when the lawyer who had kept him out of jail was himself forced to flee to Brazil after being involved in the murder of a seventeen-year-old boy. Burroughs Jnr had been sent to St Louis and Joan's daughter had gone to stay with her grandparents. With few friends and less money, Burroughs decided not to take his chances with a Mexican court. He left Mexico in December 1952 and spent six months in South America searching out Yage – a quest that, this time, turned out to be successful. In August 1953 he left Mexico for good, passing through Palm Beach to see his parents and then going on to New York to meet up with Ginsberg, with whom he would edit *The Yage Letters*, and Gregory Corso.

Whilst Burroughs had been entangled in the nightmare of Mexico, Ginsberg had been acting as his unofficial literary agent in New York. During a stint in a psychiatric hospital at Columbia, Ginsberg had befriended a fellow-patient called Carl Solomon – a name that would later be immortalized by having 'Howl' dedicated

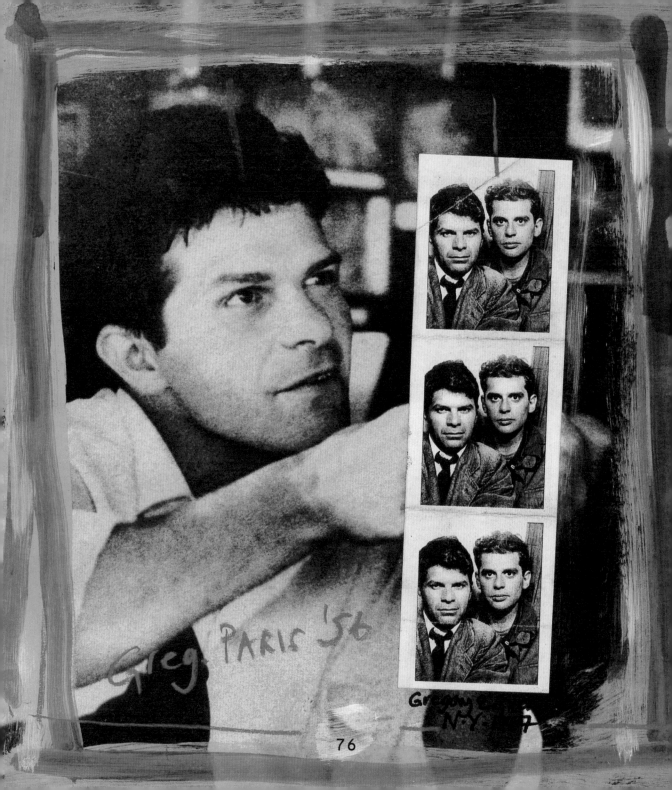

Greg. PARIS '56

Gregory Corso
N·Y·47

to him. On Solomon's release he took a job with his uncle, A. A. Wyn, who published Ace Books. Wyn was interested in publishing *Junkie*, particularly as the reformed-druggie genre had been made fashionable by Nelson Algren's *The Man With The Golden Arm* in 1949. By the time Ace had committed themselves to the projects Burroughs had begun work on his second novel, *Queer*. Wyn became insistent that he should include chapters from the second book along with the first, and withheld the $800 advance in an attempt to get him to agree. After various deliberations, Burroughs included forty pages of *Queer* and in May 1953 100,000 copies of *Junkie* appeared. Partly to distance themselves from accusations of drugs promotion, and partly out of commercial expediency, the novel was published between the same covers as the memoirs of a narcotics agent as part of the Ace Double-Book series.

In September 1953 Burroughs returned to New York to meet up with Ginsberg and his new friend Gregory Corso (left).

Junkie generated little interest when it was published, and Burroughs subsequently dismissed it as trivia. Yet the book does provide a blueprint for many of his later concerns. The project may be what he called 'comparatively simple: to put down in the most accurate and simple terms my experience as an addict', though this summary underplays the ways in which his novel captures the dead-pan laconic drawl of the junkiesphere. His prose does not simply describe the heroin lifestyle, it mimics it. In its detached understatement the narrative enacts its own autism. Bill Lee is not the subject of the novel, but its object; a character with no inner life who recounts his progression through four habits and his search for Yage – the junkie's Holy Grail. The stunned, anaesthetized voice that he adopts speaks from within the junk condition as well as about it – a technique that would later inform the work of writers such as Joan Didion and Bret Easton Ellis.

Junkie

BY THE AUTHOR OF 'THE NAKED LUNCH'

William Burroughs

Junkie held up a mirror to the grotesque well-being of the 1950s – a decade of consumer frenzy and self-satisfied affluence. To a culture driven by conspicuous consumption does not junk become the ultimate merchandise – a product that crystallizes the most brutal imperatives of supply and demand? In equating identity with addiction and conformity with control, *Junkie* suggests not so much a deviation from society as its logical culmination. 'I have learned the junk equation,' he was to write in the book's prologue. 'Junk is not a kick. It is a way of life.' It was an ironic epitaph to a decade that spent more on advertising than it did on education.

Burroughs's visit with Allen Ginsberg in New York proved to be a poisoned chalice. On the one hand their friendship had matured into genuine soulmatery. The mentor–pupil dynamic had been replaced by a more equal exchange of emotional and intellectual depth. As Ginsberg wrote to Neal Cassady, 'I'm older now and the emotional relationship and conflict of will and mutual digging are very intense, continuous, exhausting and fertile....I come home from work at 4.45 and we talk until one AM or later. I hardly get enuf sleep, can't think about work seriously, am hung up in great psychic marriage with him.' It was here that they edited and shaped what would later become *The Yage Letters* and also, at Kerouac's suggestion, they began to discuss ideas for a book to be called *The Naked Lunch*.

On the other hand, Burroughs fell hopelessly in love with the younger man and began to crowd him with his suffocating need. This is the first time their friendship had become sexual, and to begin with Ginsberg was both casual and flattered. As he recalled, 'Burroughs fell

THE
MAN
WITH
THE
GOLDEN
ARM

A film by Otto Preminger

NOVEL '49
MOVIE '55

American

JOAN 77

BRET '86

4/1/77-NEW YORK: Joan Didion's new novel, "A Book of Common Prayer" is set in California and Central America and is tuned to the currents of several kinds of revolution. Published by Simon and Schuster, the book has been called a "remarkable modern variation on Henry James' "The Portrait of a Lady." Tennessee Williams said of Didion and her book: "a completely knowing and sophisticated grasp of realities and all unrealities in our time and place, together with a lyrical treatment of them, strikes me as being the ultimate achievement of a contemporary novelist."

US writers;
BRET EASTON ELLIS
OPS Bret Easton Ellis, the controversial US fiction writer who set a precedent for destructive and depressing comment on American life with *Less Than Zero* (1986) centred around the decadent lifestyle of a group of rich young Californians, written at the tender age of 21. Since then he has gone on to incite ever greater numbers of readers with *Rules of Attraction* and by far the most controversial (and obscene) *American Psycho*.

in love with me and we slept together…and since I did love him and did have that respect and affection, he responded. I kinda felt privileged.' For Burroughs their affair was more serious and he began to talk of 'schlupping' – a state in which two people merged into one entity, possessing the other by dissolving into him. Ginsberg moved from being privileged to running scared: 'Bill became more and more demanding that there be some kind of mental schlupp. It had gone beyond the point of being humorous or playful. It seemed that Bill was demanding it for real. Bill wanted a relationship where there were no holds barred; to achieve an ultimate telepathic union of souls.'

Left: The reformed-druggie genre had been made fashionable by Nelson Algren's The Man With the Golden Arm *in 1949. Techniques from* Junkie *would later inform the work of writers such as Joan Didion and Bret Easton Ellis.*

Things came to a head when Burroughs tried to persuade him to move to Tangier. 'But I don't want your ugly old cock,' Ginsberg responded, with brutal honesty that cut Burroughs deeply. 'It wounded him terribly,' recalls Ginsberg, 'because it was like complete physical rejection in a way I didn't mean. Like a heart blow that severed the trust, because I'd freaked out for that moment and regretted it ever since.' Burroughs left for Tangier, Ginsberg for California. It had been a bitter-sweet experience for both of them.

When Burroughs arrived in Morocco in January 1954 he found a place awash with the kind of bohemian laxity of which he had only dreamt. Hashish was smoked in the streets, hard drugs were sold over the counter, policing was minimal, homosexuality carried no taboo and pederasty seemed to be almost actively encouraged, not least by the Tangier boys themselves. A large ex-pat community had sprung up there, giving the place a sense of transience and instability. As Burroughs wrote to Ginsberg, 'There is an end-of-the-world feeling in Tangier, with its glut of nylon shirts, Swiss watches, Scotch and sex and opiates sold across the counter. Something sinister in complete laissez-faire.'

TANGIER
1961

TANGER, MAROC

A LADY
OF MOROCCO

NGIER 1957

ORLOVSKY,
KEROUAC
W·S·B →

82

Yet for all its exotic danger, Burroughs was desperately unhappy in Tangier. He was frantically writing to Ginsberg and failing to get any reply. In a letter to Kerouac he compares his need for Ginsberg with his addiction to heroin, and certainly the correspondence of this time has all the urgency of a junkie tracking down the Man. 'I did not think I was hooked on him like this,' he wrote in April 1954. 'The withdrawal symptoms are worse than the Marker habit. One letter would fix me. So make it your business, if you are a real friend, to see that he writes me a fix. I am incapacitated. Can't write. Can't take an interest in anything.'

Tangier, Morocco, in 1954 was awash with bohemian laxity. Hashish was smoked in the streets, hard drugs were sold over the counter, policing was minimal and homosexuality carried no taboo.

In Ginsberg's absence he began relying heavily on Eukodol, a derivative of codeine which could be acquired over the counter. His room at 1 Calle de los Arcos was conveniently situated above a male brothel and one of the prostitutes working there – a young Spanish boy called Kiki – became a constant companion. Ginsberg had renewed contact, which gave him the friendship fix he had needed so badly as well as an ideal reader for the routines he had begun producing again. Many of these literary riffs found their way into *The Naked Lunch* – the talking asshole routine most famously. His letters to Ginsberg were in effect a form of collaboration, a way of testing the boundaries of an idea or image by creating for himself an implied audience. As with Kells Elvins, Kerouac and later Gysin, Burroughs found in Ginsberg a way of exploring the demons in himself through the critical eyes of someone else. As he acknowledged in a letter to Ginsberg, 'I have to have receiver for routine. If there is no one there to receive it, routine turns back on me and tears me apart, grows more and more insane (literal growth like cancer) and impossible, and fragmentary like berserk pinball machine and I am screaming "Stop it! Stop it!"' Writing had thus become a form of psycho-drama, with Ginsberg as both critic and analyst. Tangier began to translate itself in his writing into Interzone – the demi-monde of *The Naked Lunch* with himself as its most ambivalent tour guide.

Morocco may have unleashed his creativity, but the availability of drugs was incapacitating him all the more. By the end of his first year there he was shooting Eukadol every two hours and even pawning his typewriter to buy drugs. 'I never had a habit like this before,' he wrote Ginsberg. 'Trust the Germans to concoct some really evil shit....A shot of Eukadol hits the head first with a rush of pleasure. Ten minutes later you want another shot. Between shots you are just killing time.'

By the beginning of 1956 the situation had become desperate. Repeated attempts at gradual withdrawal either failed entirely or ended in relapse within a couple of weeks. In February he borrowed $500 from his parents and went to London to undergo the apomorphine cure pioneered by Dr John Yerbury Dent. Dent had discovered the potential of apomorphine in his treatment of alcoholism, and realized that its ability to regulate the metabolism could be used to equal effect for other addictions. Burroughs discussed his treatment in his 'Letter from a Master Addict to Dangerous Drugs', first published in the *British Journal of Addiction* and later reprinted as an appendix to *The Naked Lunch*. More importantly, the cure was successful and in September he returned to Tangier clean. As he was to remark later, '[apomorphine was] the turning point between life and death. I would never have been cured without it. *Naked Lunch* would never have been written.'

'Trust the Germans to concoct some really evil shit.'

Following pages: Ginsberg and Burroughs began to discuss ideas for a book to be called *The Naked Lunch*. It was published in 1959 by Olympia Press, with Grove following suit in 1962.

Upon his return Burroughs moved into the Villa Muniria and immersed himself in a new regime of furious writing and recreational hashish. As he wrote to Ginsberg, 'Interzone is coming like dictation. I can't keep up with it', adding later, 'This is almost automatic writing. I often sit high on hash for as long as six hours typing at top speed.' Hash replaced narcotics, leaving Burroughs feeling healthier, even nearly happy, and he began socializing with the Tangier intelligentsia who had remained distant whilst he was on junk.

Ever since his arrival in 1948 Paul Bowles had established himself at the centre of the Tangier literary set – his experiences there are perhaps best recorded in his autobiography, *Without Stopping*. Like Burroughs he was a homosexual who had married, his wife being the precociously talented Jane Auer. Yet their initial meetings had revealed little common ground. Bowles recalls his first encounter with Burroughs being clouded with the latter's strung-out dissolution and gun fetishism. For his part Burroughs regarded Bowles as stuffy and reserved. To Ginsberg he labelled him 'a shameless faker', whilst to Kerouac he complained, 'The one time I met Paul Bowles he evinced no cordiality. Since then he has made no effort to follow up the acquaintance....He invites the dreariest queens in Tangier to tea but has never invited me, which, seeing how small the town is, amounts to a deliberate affront.'

Yet after the cure their friendship came good: Bowles provided him with literary encouragement and access to Tangier society. In December 1956 Burroughs wrote to Ginsberg that Bowles was 'one of the really great people I meet in last three years....Don't recall I ever meet anyone I dug so quick as Bowles.' It is ironic that it was through Bowles that Burroughs met Brion Gysin – another person to

Poet Ginsberg Defends 'Naked Lunch'

and nasty, sprawled on a Florida beach surrounded
by simpering blond

This citizen may
China! He figure to
Xmas TV short to
pes-
real McCoy, but that Latah get up in lewd state
and put on his Santa Claus suit and make with the
switcheroo. Come the dawning. The citizen put
one rope on and the Latah, going along the way
Latahs will, put on the other. When the traps are
down the citizen hang for real and the Latah stand
with the carny-rubber stretch rope. Well, the Latah
imitate every twitch and spasm. Come three
times.

"Smart young Latah keep his eye on the ball.
ot him working in one of my plants as an expe
itor."

blue eather robe

"But where is the st
side of his face, the ou
of a Million Mirrors.
Queen Bee continue
nothing.

Couches, chairs, t
vibrate, shaking the g
shrieking in cock-bou

Two boys jacking o
train shakes through
fades with distant w
wash semen off lean h

By JOSEPH M. HARVEY

The trial of the controversial book "Naked Lunch" came to a close Wednesday in Suffolk Superior Court on a poetic note.

Bearded, bespectacled Alan Ginsberg, a poet from Greenwich Village was the final witness in a parade of college English professors and psychiatrists before Judge Eugene Hudson. Judge Hudson took under advisement the suit by Atty. Gen. Edward W. Brooke which seeks to have the book burned in Massachusetts as obscene.

The book by William Burroughs, first published in English in Paris in 1959, sets out in "gutter talk" the experiences of a drug addict. Ginsburg likened Burroughs' writing to that of Ezra Pound and T. S. Eliot.

Asked by Judge Hudson to explain the title, Ginsberg said it meant "The nakedness of seeing, to be able to see clearly, to see through disguises." "The lunch, Ginsberg said, "is a banquet of all this naked awareness." He said Burroughs in the book satirized capital punishment, political parties, and gives a "scientific discourse" on modern brain

washing and police state tactics. He said Burroughs wrote on the "Algebra of need" and on the United States addition to materialistic goods, property, money, and to power by controlling other people."

One of the final witnesses was Prof. Thomas B. Jackson of Newton, professor of English at Massachusetts Institute of Technology. He likened the book to Dante's "Inferno."

When Judge Hudson asked Jackson if he "knew of any obscene words or expressions that do not appear in this book," Jackson paused for a moment, then stand.

ALAN GINSBERG

"I heard one, once," Jackson testified

keeps eguards carry in iron-lungs full of para-
yzed youths.

bleeding for the black
your mother, rimmed
ing around so nasty

rise from a black pond
wards on the surface).

d dress shirt, naked from
black garters, talks to
es. (Queen Bees are
emselves with fairie
nister Mexican practi
ary?" He talks out of
is twisted by the Te
masturbates wildly.
he conversation, no

whole floor beg
ts to blurred grey
agony.

der railroad bridg
r bodies, ejaculate
e. Frogs croak. The boys
n stomachs.

wo sick young junkies on
tear their pants down in
of them soaps his cock
er's ass with a corkscrew
esus!" Both ejaculate at
r move away from each
nts.

all writes for tincture and

other shriek out raw and
t. . . . Doc, suppose it was
resident leaches, squirm-

Let's stop over and make him for an R
The train tears on through the smoky ne
lighted June night.

women, boys and girls, a
opulating rhythm of t e u
verse flows through he room, a great blue le
dless hum of deep st
es when the junky c p s.
and wonder. Even the o
buzzes clogged lines of cholesterol for co

out: "This is your doing
rty!"

him, face remote as lime n
you liquefying gook."

mad American women rush
from farm and dude ranch, f
ry, brother, country club, penthouse and subur
motel and yacht and ocktail bar, strip off ridi
clothes, ski togs, evening dresses, levis tea gow
print dr suits and kimone
They s eap on the gue
like bit hey claw at it
hanged You bastar
Fuck The guests fl
screamin boys, ov
turn iro
A.J.: Can out my Sweitzers, God damn
Guard me from these he-foxes!"
Mr. Hyslop, A.J. ecretary, looks up from
comic book: "The Sweitzers liquefy already."
(Liquefaction involves protein cleavage and

'Beat' became a
literary
sensation.
'Howl' was
published in
1956 to a
mixture of
outrage and
acclaim, with
Ginsberg's
coast-to-coast
readings of the
poem generating
the electric
atmosphere of a
rock
performance.
The following
year Kerouac
signed his
contract for *On
the Road*.

whom there was immediate antipathy, yet who would later become a lifelong friend. When Bowles invited Gysin to tea with Burroughs their conversation was awkward, stilted and competitive. 'Impossible, impossible,' said Gysin to Bowles. 'I know, I've seen him staggering around. He's just an old junky.' It was not until several years later that these two would discover their legendary chemistry.

Tangier may have been transformed into what Burroughs called 'the most beautiful city in the world', and his junk-free phase was certainly his most productive to date. Even after the cure and his acceptance into artistic Tangier, he still required the hands-on help of his Columbia friends. As early as 1955 Burroughs was writing to Ginsberg, 'I need you so much your absence causes me, at times, acute pain....I mean in conjunction with my writing. I think I am at the point of jumping in the lake instead of skirting the edges, and feel a great need for your help at this critical juncture.' His friends arrived in Tangier in the spring of 1957.

By this time 'Beat' had become a literary sensation, the word speaking to a condition that was angelic in its disaffection – both 'Beaten' and 'Beatific'. 'Howl' had been published in 1956 to a mixture of outrage and acclaim, with Ginsberg's coast-to-coast readings of the poem generating the electric atmosphere of a rock performance. Kerouac had signed his contract for *On the Road* in January 1957, and newspaper editorials buzzed with both moral panic and prurient interest about the influence of these artistic hobos. It is significant that Burroughs should have been exiled in Tangier when the Beat phenomenon made big in the States. His geographical distance also suggests an aesthetic one. The touchstone of Beat was a defiant naïveté – a stubborn refusal to allow their songs of innocence to be stifled by their experience of corporate America. Against a world of bovine maturity and faceless conformity they sought to unleash the potential of the moment, finding it in the orgasm, in jazz and in their communal solipsism.

Burroughs's writing, however, is never an overture to the 'oversoul', nor to any notion of the unfettered ego.

As his routines to Ginsberg and then *The Naked Lunch* were to reveal, Burroughs was less interested in side-stepping systems of control than in exploding them from within. His writing dramatizes the various locations of power, examining how they converge and conflict, cannibalizing themselves in pursuit of their own totality. Whereas a writer like Kerouac was to deify the blacks, finding in their oppression a metaphor for his own lost yearnings ('wishing I was a Negro, feeling that the best the white world had offered was not enough ecstasy for me'), Burroughs instead parodied the psycho-pathology of a racist establishment. It was not the glamour of racial invisibility that intrigued Burroughs, but the mind-set that created it. The Beats produced alternative ideologies; Burroughs looked at how we are produced by them.

His association with the Beats was, however, crucial in shaping and ultimately publishing his second book. Kerouac arrived in Tangier first, landing in February 1957 and taking a room above Burroughs's in the Villa Muniria. A competent typist, he worked for six hours a day on Burroughs's manuscript so that he eventually had 'nightmares of great long baloneys coming out of my mouth'. A month later Ginsberg arrived with his new lover, Peter Orlovsky, and their friend

Burroughs tried to persuade Ginsberg to move to Tangier. 'But I don't want your ugly old cock,' Ginsberg responded.

Alan Ansen soon joined them from Venice. The group did not quite gel as expected. Kerouac shipped out in early April, whilst Burroughs expressed his jealousy of Orlovsky with bitchy quips and an ice-cold shoulder. Yet by June the novel had taken most of the form in which it was to be published. Ansen, Orlovsky and Ginsberg left for Spain,

leaving Burroughs to fine-tune his work and finish the Benway section. 'It's quite a piece of writing,' wrote Ginsberg to Lucien Carr, 'all Bill's energy & prose, plus our organization & cleanup & structure.' With the Beat set having gone, Burroughs took a trip to Copenhagen to visit Kells Elvins. It was here that he developed the 'Freeland' section of *The Naked Lunch*, finding the place so profoundly tedious that 'no other place could be the background' for a city that 'exceeds my most ghastly imaginings'.

Returning to Tangier, he cut himself off from everyone and submerged himself in the completing of the project. 'I do nothing but work,' he wrote to Ginsberg. 'Writing the narrative now, which comes in great hunks faster than I can get it down. Changes in psyche are profound and basic....Nothing but work and weed all day.' As his writing took precedence, Burroughs's affection for Tangier waned, until he began to see the city as actively hostile. He wrote that 'The place is plague-ridden', and that the boys and the drugs no longer had any appeal.

Three years later, Ginsberg arrived — with his new lover, Peter Orlovsky.

On 4 December 1957 he wrote to Kerouac that he was planning 'to join Allen in Paris', and by January of the following year he had done so.

Chapter 6

In their exodus to Paris, Burroughs and the Beats were following in a literary tradition of exiled Americans – a lineage that stretches from Henry James and Scott Fitzgerald through to Richard Wright and James Baldwin. Gertrude Stein had prophetically remarked that 'It is I an American who was and is thinking and writing in America and lives in Paris. This has been and probably will be the history of the world.' She was not far wrong. Indeed the apartment that Ginsberg found for them – 9 rue Git Le Coeur – had been occupied the year before by Chester Himes, the Black Negro to Mailer's 'White'. The Beat Hotel, as it would later be canonized, was described by one journalist as a 'fleabag shrine where passersby move out of the way for rats', yet it proved to be a productive environment for the Americans, who found in it an echo of their years at Columbia (with Corso replacing Kerouac).

The infamous Olympia Press seemed the most obvious home for a book like Burroughs's, and Ginsberg approached them through one of their editors, Sinclair Beiles. Founded in 1953 by Maurice Girodias, Olympia had gained its notoriety by publishing the obscure, the pornographic and the transgressive. Girodias had

Par avion

Paris

94

WILLIAM BURROUGHS
THE NAKED LUNCH

Paris in the fifties was the obvious home for a book like *The Naked Lunch*, a collage of comic-strip surrealism, sexuality and sadism.

already notched up De Sade, Bataille, Henry Miller and Alexander Trocchi to his credit, and was encouraging the last of these to write pseudonymous porn to subsidize his more serious work. Yet Girodias at first rejected *The Naked Lunch*, claiming that the manuscript was in such a mess 'you couldn't physically read the stuff....The ends of the pages were all eaten away by rats or something.' Ginsberg sent a section of the manuscript to the *Chicago Review*, a student magazine of the city's university. Burroughs's publication caused such a stir that the editors resigned and started an independent magazine, *Big Table*, which published more of his work. The controversy that had been created was enough to force Girodias to reconsider his initial rejection and, on an advance of $1500, Olympia published the novel in 1959. Barney Rosset, the founder of Grove Press, hired Irving Rosenthal (a former *Big Table* editor) to copy-edit the book and it finally appeared in New York in 1962.

The Naked Lunch was an event as much as a novel. It became the essential purchase of the aspiring hipster, particularly in Britain where copies had to be smuggled through customs. It was 'cult' incarnate - an underground collage of comic-strip surrealism which juxtaposed sexuality with sadism, business with crime and politics with madness to the extent that such terms became interchangeable. *The Naked Lunch* was almost instantly iconic – a signifier of its own vagrancy.

Relations between Burroughs and Ginsberg were no longer fraught with sexual tension – Burroughs had begun to warm to Orlovsky, prompting Ginsberg to write to him, 'He no longer needs me like he used to, he doesn't think of me as a permanent future intimate sex schlupp lover.' In fact Burroughs was undergoing

BRION GYSIN SUCKING ON BIG TOE (ONLY HAS FOUR TOES) 1978

psycho-analysis and was beginning to re-evaluate his entire attitude to sex, reporting to Ginsberg that '[I] don't know if I am interested in man or woman or both or neither. I think neither. Just can't dig the natives on this planet.'

The Beat Hotel played host to the cream of Parisian bohemia, the Beats' ascendant celebrity bringing them into contact with figures such as Man Ray, Céline and Marcel Duchamp. One of Burroughs's most significant encounters, however, was with a less well-known artist – a bisexual, British-born painter called Brion Gysin. Although Gysin had run a restaurant in Tangier, the two men had found little common ground there. But in Paris their friendship flourished as they discovered a shared interest in conspiracy, magic, altered states and misogyny. They became fascinated by the eleventh-century

One of Burroughs's most significant encounters in Paris was with a bisexual, British-born painter called Brion Gysin. Photographed here in LA, 1978.

Persian sect known as the Assassins, whose leader, Hassan I Sabbah, arrived at the maxim, 'Nothing is true, everything is permitted.' This was to become their aesthetic code of conduct, and certainly underpins their use of the cut-up.

When Ginsberg returned to America, Gysin took his place in the Beat Hotel. Burroughs has always credited Gysin with discovering the cut-up, although the Dada poet Tristan Tzara had caused a riot decades earlier when he composed a poem by pulling words out of a hat. Whatever its origins, the cut-up can be seen as a logical extension of their mutual trajectory. In *The Naked Lunch* Burroughs had used writing against itself, commandeering language so that it might 'Rub out The Word'. The critic Tony Tanner has compared this prose to the music of John Cage, whose random (sometimes silent) compositions cause us to reassess the pact between composer and audience and the relationship between authority and structure. As Burroughs put it, 'Cut-ups destroy old false constructs and models of reality', while Gysin called the experiments 'a project

Peter ORLOVSKY and Allen GINSBERG in Rue St-André-des-Arts, December 1956. At that time they were living in Room 25 of the Beat Hotel PARIS.

98

for disastrous success'. Burroughs's many collaborations with Gysin represent the War of the Words — an assault on the imprisoning totality of language by celebrating the random, a word's chance encounter with its own free-floating status. Just as we do not listen to Cage's silences, we do not read the Burroughs/Gysin books. They are textual tantrums that need to be approached as concepts, not as narratives. To disregard them as 'unreadable' is no more helpful than disagreeing with a joke or a riddle.

Whilst Burroughs was exploring new possibilities for writing, *The Naked Lunch* was becoming the subject of a narrative all to itself. On 20 January 1962 a bookseller in Boston was arrested on obscenity charges for selling copies of the book. The trial was set for two years later and the defence called both academics and writers to

Left: Orlovsky and Ginsberg, Paris, December 1956.

testify to the book's merits. John Ciardi, poetry editor of *Saturday Review*, praised 'a substantial work by an author of some talent and of serious commitment', whilst Norman Mailer spoke of an 'artistry...more deliberate and more profound than I thought before'. Ginsberg was also called and discussed the function of addiction as a metaphor for social critique. Their testimonies fell on deaf ears and the book was found to be obscene. It was only on appeal, handed down on 7 July 1966, that the verdict went in the publisher's favour, thus marking the end of (official) literary censorship in America.

The avant-garde British literary publisher John Calder was more cautious, understandably wary of an establishment who could ask whether or not we should allow our wives and servants to read D. H. Lawrence. In August 1962, he organized a conference in Edinburgh to address the question 'How does the novel form stand today?' Over seventy writers were invited, including Mailer, Mary McCarthy,

UGH . . .

WILLIAM BURROUGHS : *The Naked Lunch*. 226pp. 15fr. *The Soft Machine*. 182pp. 15fr. *The Ticket That Exploded*. 183pp.—18fr.—Paris : Olympia Press.
WILLIAM BURROUGHS : *Dead Fingers Talk*. 215pp. John Calder. 25s.

" Now I, William Seward, will unlock my word horde ", warns Mr. Burroughs towards the end of *The Naked Lunch*. Struggling upstream through it is not unlike wading through the drains of a big city. The first shock effects are strong as the rash reader plunges in, then a steady nausea follows which hangs around him long after he has fought his way into the fresh air,—finally boredom with the endless monotony as he tries to pick up his stinking feet and skip. Look out : here it comes !

From the open bronze mold emerged a transparent green shape criss-crossed with pulsing red veins, liquid screen eyes swept by color flashes—A smell of sewage and decay breathing from years of torture films, orgasm death in his black eyes glinting with the slow fish lust of the swamp mud—Long tendril hands penetrated Bradly's broken body caressing the other being inside through the soft intestines into the pearly genitals rubbing centers of orgasm along his spine up to the neck—Exquisite toothache pain shot through his nerves and his body split down the middle—Sex word, exploded to a poisonous color vapor that cut off his breath. . . .

On and on it flows, lapping slowly round what soon becomes a stereotyped debris : ectoplasm, jelly, errand boys, ferris wheels, used contraceptives, centipedes, old photographs, jockstraps, turnstiles, newts and pubic hairs.

Such is the texture of the grey porridge in which Mr. Burroughs specializes. Three brimming books which he has filled with it for the Olympia Press have already attracted some speculative attention among those who have not read them, partly because of their excellent (though irrelevant) titles, partly because of the respectful admiration of one or two half-stupefied critics, but above all by their blacklisting by the British Customs and the U.S. Mails. Now the author himself has fished out an assortment of lumps from all three, stirring the mixture and topping it up to make a fourth, slightly more hygienic bucketful which can be cast before us swine.

Glug glug. It tastes disgusting, even without the detailed but always callous homosexual scenes and the unspeakable homosexual fantasies— pure verbal masturbation—that figure so largely in the Olympia Press volumes. Ye ... ... are perfectly intelligent supporters of these books

who see them as a deliberate indictment of the society we live in : as a satire on the American Way of Life, a great comic saga of the world below the navel, or a nightmare account of the drug addictions through which the author has passed. How far this can be held to make such a diet agreeable or nutritious is another matter, but it is quite true that Mr. Burroughs's writing gives some insight into the world of drugs, both by islets of straight description (as in the opening of *The Naked Lunch*, which is also the opening of the Calder volume)—and by suggesting how the imagination and perceptions are affected. It frequently moves into a kind of farcical high gear, the charade-like style that a number of juxtaposition like articles abandoned in a hotel drawer, defined by negatives and absences . . . .

What this amounts to is montage, piecing a book together from disjointed chunks that can be satire or parody or else like the unplanned dribbling and splashing of the action painter. Far from having any " total fabric " in mind, the author can reshuffle the pieces and make a " new " book, or the individual chunk can be broken down into phrases and sorted and scattered so that the words come tumbling out in a new order and the already familiar sentences slide out of focus.

This is not a bad way of conveying the mental mists of what Mr. Burroughs terms " the pick-up frontier, a languid grey area of hiatus miasmic with yawns and gaping goof holes " (a zone he clearly knows well), while the repetitiveness to which it leads is only too natural to an author whose best phrases anyway tend to recur (the subway sweeping by " with a black blast of iron ", for instance), and whose images and adjectives— like " obsidian "—are often overworked. But it is not always clear whether it is the writing or the writer that is being jumbled, while the air of pretentiousness which surrounds the whole business (aggravated by the author's readings on tape and a ridiculous short film) by no means excuses monotony and impoverishment of style. A yawn is a yawn is a yawn, the reader soon comes to feel. The technique is of a piece with the material all right, but only in the sense

that without the shocks and the stench there would be nothing much left.

" Montons la pompe à merde ", says the old French army song. Well, now it has been mounted here, to produce lunch for the British. Sample menu :

The Clear Camel Piss Soup with boiled Earth Worms

The Filet of Sun-Ripened Sting Ray basted with Eau de Cologne and garnished with nettles

The After-Birth Suprême de Boeuf cooked in drained crank case oil served with a piquant sauce of rotten egg yolks and crushed bed bugs

The Limburger Cheese sugar cured in diabetic urine doused in Canned Heat Flamboyant

—as one of the supposedly comic chunks in the new house-trained version has it. A delicious prospect, especially considering the second helpings that another sieving-through of the material might produce. If the publishers had deliberately set out to discredit the cause of literary freedom and innovation they could hardly have done it more effectively. Let us hope that they are left to appreciate the probable impact on their own reputation, and indirectly on that of the other authors on their list, without any interfering body turning them into martyrs. Any juryman can vomit, but only one verdict can clear up the mess : that of the book world itself.

writers have borrowed from Joyce's Nighttown ; while *The Ticket That Exploded* is written partly (though by no means predominantly) as a parody of science fiction. On the strength of such qualities it can be argued, as *The Saturday Review* once put it, that " the obscenities—if obscenities they are—are inseparable from the total fabric and effect of the moral message ".

But is there a moral message ? And how about if the moral message is itself disgusting ? The texture of the passages of farce or satire is in fact very much the same as that of the porridge, even if it is now being chucked around for comic effect ; most of them moreover are directed not against the junk world but against the doctors, policemen, psy-chiatrists and officials with whom the

addict and the homosexual have to deal. They are seldom set in the United States, taking place rather in Mexico, Tangier, the Latin American republics or other areas closer associated with the expatriate's than with the American way of life. Nor do the most shocking episodes seem to be put forward in a particularly satirical spirit : like this relatively printable one from *The Naked Lunch*, for instance—

Met Marv in front of the Sargasso with two Arab kids and he said :
" Want to watch these two kids screw each other ? "

" Of course. How much ? "

" I think they will perform for fifty cents. Hungry, you know."

" That's the way I like to see them." Made me feel like a dirty old man but " Son cosas de la vida " . . .—

a comment meaning " life's like that ". Or take the attitude to the young or relapsed addict, as seen in *The Soft Machine*—

I handed him two nickels under the table. Pushing in a small way to keep up The Habit : INVADE. DAMAGE. OCCUPY. Young faces in blue alcohol flame.

At the very least, such things are too uncritically presented, and because the author gives no flicker of disapproval the reader easily takes the " moral message " to lie the other way.

In *Dead Fingers Talk* two of the author's farcical quacks are themselves arguing about the question of disgust :

SCHAFER : " I tell you I can't escape a feeling—well, of evil about this."

BENWAY : " Balderdash, my boy— We're scientists—Pure scientists. Disinterested research and damned be him who cries ' Hold, too much ! ' . . ."

SCHAFER : " Yes, yes, of course—and yet—I can't get that stench out of my lungs."

There are Benways in the literary laboratory who feel that Mr. Burroughs's characteristic stench is justified by the solemn new " fold-in " technique by which he claims to compose his books. " You can cut into Naked Lunch at any intersection point ", he says, and again in the same work :

The word cannot be expressed direct . . . It can perhaps be indicated by mosaic

WHITHER UGH

There was a simple point in the original "Ugh" by Mr. William Burroughs even wordy weeks ago...

A review entitled 'Ugh' was the beginning of a thirteen-week-long correspondence. What it lacked in literary acuity the 'Ugh Correspondence' made up for in publicity, and Calder published *The Naked Lunch* in 1964.

Henry Miller and Burroughs himself. McCarthy gave a spirited defence of *The Naked Lunch*, claiming that it 'has some of the qualities of Action Painting. It is a kind of Action Novel.' (She would echo these sentiments a few months later in a review for the *New York Review of Books* in which she compared Burroughs to a vaudeville performer playing...in front of the asbestos curtain of some Keith Circuit or Pantages house long since converted to movies'.) Mailer typically played devil's advocate and floated the idea that too much contemporary fiction was immoral in its refusal to 'enter this terrible borderland of sex, sadism, obscenity, horror, and anything else...that is why I salute Mr Burroughs' work, because he has gone further into it than any other Western writer today'. Burroughs was called upon to give his opinion on censorship and argued that if it 'were removed, perhaps books would be judged more on literary merit, and a dull, poorly written book on a sexual subject would find few readers....The anxiety and prurience of which censorship is the overt political expression has so far prevented any serious scientific investigation of sexual phenomena.'

The event put Burroughs firmly on the map and convinced Calder to produce a 'reader' – a book that contained sections from *The Naked Lunch*, as well as from *The Soft Machine* and *The Ticket that Exploded* which were also produced in the early sixties.

This selection was published in 1963 under the title *Dead Fingers Talk*. Neither work was brought before the court, but that other bastion of the British establishment, the *Times Literary Supplement*, declared war instead. John Willett instigated proceedings with a review entitled 'Ugh' – a scathing attack on what he saw as

WILLIAM BURROUGHS: (1914 -)
AMERICAN WRITER, AUTHOR OF "NAKED LUNCH"
PHOTOGRAPH TAKEN IN A PARIS BAR, 1962.

102

VALUABLE ORIGINAL
MUST BE RETURNED
BY JAN 15 1965

12-4 William S. Burroughs at a Grove Press book party on December 22, 1964. In Kerouac's novels Burroughs is identified as Will Dennison, Will Hubbard, and Frank Carmody, and in *On the Road* as Old Bull Lee.

Burroughs's sordid fascination with bodily functions, disease and sexual deviance. It was the beginning of a thirteen-week-long correspondence that included Anthony Burgess and Michael Moorcock for the defence as well as the moral outrage of Dame Edith Sitwell and the publisher Victor Gollancz, who characterized the books as 'bogus high-brow filth'. What it lacked in literary acuity the 'Ugh Correspondence' made up for in publicity, and Calder published *The Naked Lunch* in 1964.

Reading the book today, one is struck by just how eerily contemporary Burroughs's landscapes proved to be. His fantasy of a sexually transmitted disease that nourishes itself off contact with strangers was an uncanny prophecy of our own AIDS-conscious culture. The film-maker David Cronenberg once remarked that he had been making movies about AIDS long before AIDS had been discovered, so it is hardly surprising that he should eventually choose to film a novel that fits the same bill for his explorations of invasion and decay. The hyper-reality of many of the novel's routines foreshadows what postmodernism would later term the 'simulacrum', the point at which the authenticity of our experience dissolves all around us and we become consumers of our own reality. For a novel written through the fifties and published in the sixties, *The Naked Lunch* stands as one of the most astute chronicles of the nineties.

Grove
New York, NY

The Naked Lunch became the subject of a narrative all to itself, putting Burroughs firmly on the map.

Hardcover and paperback trade fiction and nonfiction titles, with major emphasis on drama, foreign literature in translation, and new fiction.

7

Chapter 7

Back in Paris, Burroughs had become involved with a young English student named Ian Sommerville – a Cambridge mathematician who was spending his vacation fixing the electrics for a Parisian bookstore. This was the first time since Ginsberg that Burroughs had allowed himself to become emotionally as well as sexually involved with someone, and this time his affections were returned. Burroughs introduced his lover to a whole new world of literature, acting as teacher, mentor and facilitator. Sommerville repaid him by becoming a technical adviser to Gysin's and Burroughs's experiments with tape-recorders and photographs – skills that would be acknowledged by Sommerville's appearances as 'The Subliminal Kid' in *The Ticket that Exploded* and 'Technical Tilly' in *Nova Express*. Their relationship lasted, with varying degrees of involvement, until Sommerville's death in 1976, and was always looked upon by Burroughs as one of the most intimate friendships of his life. Sommerville returned to Corpus Christi, Cambridge in 1960 and, with rumours that he was to be deported because of his drug connections, Burroughs moved to London to be near him, keeping up the Beat Hotel as a base.

Once he had settled in Earl's Court, Burroughs was forced to pay another visit to Dr Dent to kick a codeine habit he had developed in Paris. As with his first cure, the apomorphine treatment unleashed a

Dada poet Tristan Tzara.

These pages: Burroughs and Gysin collaborations. The pair became fascinated by the eleventh-century Persian sect known as the Assassins, whose maxim was, 'Nothing is true, everything is permitted.' This was to become the aesthetic code underpinning the cut-up technique. Previous page: Burroughs always credited Gysin with discovering the cut-up, although the Dada poet Tristan Tzara caused a riot decades earlier when he composed a poem by pulling words out of a hat.

110

new phase of creativity and, in between trips to Tangier and New York, he began frantically arranging the material that would become the 'Nova Trilogy'. Using the notes he had taken in Morocco, between 1961 and 1964 Burroughs produced three novels – *The Soft Machine*, *The Ticket that Exploded* and *Nova Express*. He had utilized the cut-up with Gysin and Corso (in *Minutes to Go* and *The Exterminator*), and now the trilogy expanded its possibilities within his own fiction. Taken as a whole, the books evoke a science-fictional universe that is founded upon various methods of controls – linguistic, judicial, sexual, medical. The texts have an anarchic force all of their own, as though they were writing themselves, and have their origins in a wide range of sources – tape-recordings, folded-over reportage, phrases repeated with hypnotic regularity. In its seventeen brief chapters *The Soft Machine* plays out the ways in which our identities are enslaved by our sexual appetite, the self somehow imprisoned by the demands of the body. Our need for the other confuses our autonomy, entangling us in an economy of interdependence and the nervous quest for completion. 'Storm the reality studio' runs one of *The Soft Machine*'s refrains, and certainly the book's method of composition suggests one attempt to meet its own challenge.

Left: Ian Sommerville's photo composite 'Dyptych', circa 1962, of William S. Burroughs and Brion Gysin.

The Ticket that Exploded focuses as much on language as it does on sexuality – a novel that puts its mouth where its body is. The Nova police are omnipresent, announcing themselves through the white noise of radios, cinema and tape. The book's battle-cry is to 'Rub out the Word and the image track that goes with it' an attempt to make language the agent of its own destruction. In many ways the trilogy is a form of fictional suicide, a search-and-destroy mission whose target is the very form that created it. It would be the best part of a decade before Burroughs published another novel. He did, however, contribute widely to underground magazines during the mid-1960s, before beginning work on *The Wild Boys*.

I. — **AFRIQUE**   *Super*¹. 29 820
     O. E. = *Développ. des côtes.* 20 500
Congo, 4 700 ; Niger, 4 160 ; Zambèze, 2 660 ; Orange, 2 140. = *Tempér. extr.* Sahara
régions les plus brûlantes du globe. = *Tempér. moy.* Air tempéré (Algérie, Cap).
Air. torride, 26 à 35° C. = *Population.* 142 600 000
Sémites (Arabes, Juifs) ; Hamites (Maures, Berbères, Coptes, Éthiopiens)

Despite the fact that he was published and productive, Burroughs's mood at the beginning of the sixties was far from stable. Maurice Girodias has described 'a gray phantom of a man in his phantom gabardine and ancient discoloured phantom hat'. Ginsberg agreed, recalling that his behaviour was deeply mistrustful and his attitude misanthropic. Matters were not helped by the attentions of a seventeen-year-old English lad called Mikey Portman, whom Ginsberg described as a 'spoilt brat English Lord who looks like a palefaced Rimbaud but is a smart creep…the kid bugs everyone so intimacy with Bill is limited and Bill absentminded all the time'. Portman was gay, with an alcohol and heroin dependence, and thought he had found in Burroughs some father-like super-ego. His sycophancy was by turns flattering and infuriating – although the latter became more dominant when the young man began imitating his way of talking, tea-drinking and drug-taking. Yet Burroughs was unable to shake off his new-found groupie and Portman became a regular fixture, much to Ian Sommerville's annoyance.

In the summer of 1961 the Beat crowd reconvened in Tangier – Alan Ansen, Ginsberg, Corso and Orlovsky being joined by Burroughs, Sommerville and Portman. The atmosphere was not exactly easy – Portman irritated everyone, while Burroughs regularly baited Orlovsky, accusing him of being heterosexual, and was suspicious of Ginsberg, asking him who he was an agent for. In fact everyone appeared to him to be an agent at this point, as he wove himself into increasingly more elaborate webs of conspiracy. Women 'were a basic mistake, and the whole dualistic universe evolved from this error'; language, of course, was a virus; friendship was an illusion ('There are no friends….There are allies. There are accomplices') and love was 'a fraud perpetrated by the female sex'. The world of routines was becoming indistinguishable from reality, and Burroughs was beginning to sound like one of his own creations.

In the summer of 1961 the Beat crowd reconvened in Tangier. Photographed here at the Hotel Muniria.

It was during this period that Timothy Leary came to visit, having already corresponded with Burroughs earlier in the year about his research at Harvard into mind-altering drugs. Although both men shared a common interest in the possibilities of magic mushrooms, Burroughs remained sceptical about Leary's experiment. Leary's

evangelical nature, with his insistence on the social benefits of turning on and tuning in, was certainly at odds with Burroughs's own fascination with the mechanisms of control and the nature of addiction. His experiences with hallucinogenics had not been good, and his trip with Leary resulted in what Burroughs called 'one of the nastiest cases ever processed by this department'. He was, however, interested enough in Leary's work to fly with him to Boston and get involved in a month-long experiment with the effects of drugs on prison inmates. But again Burroughs found Leary's idealism misplaced, and he returned to London at the end of 1961 having written to Ginsberg that 'I hope never to set eyes on that horse's ass again.' It was not until 1978 that their friendship solidified; indeed, Leary spoke to Burroughs on the phone just before Leary died.

Burroughs's encounter with psychedelia is yet another example of him being both of the moment yet distanced from it. As with the Beats, his relationship with Leary was a case of having one eye on history whilst the other saw through it.

Back in London he continued to investigate the psychic possibilities of technology, with Sommerville once again acting as his scientific muse. In Paris he and Gysin had already developed the Dream Machine – a cylinder full of slits that was lit from the inside and when placed on a turntable produced rays of light at thirteen flashes per second. Burroughs believed that it possessed magical properties and was capable of inducing visions (not to mention headaches and epilepsy). He experimented exhaustively with tape-recorders, producing hundreds of hours of tapes that had been cut up from street sounds, conversations, Moroccan music, readings of his books and even people asleep. His aim was to wage war on the technological age from within the belly of the beast itself. Convinced that the mass media was an agent of control, Burroughs's response was to defamiliarize its messages, splicing and rearranging society's sounds in ways that expose their essential hollowness. As he was to recall later, 'We weren't thinking about art, we were thinking about alterations and the, shall we say, the potentialities of the tape-recorder for altering additions, and how they were undoubtedly being used for this purpose by official agencies.'

Left: Burroughs illustrated the jacket for the 1966 edition of *The Soft Machine*.

In the summer of 1962, after the Edinburgh conference, Burroughs came into contact with a British film-maker named Anthony Balch who alternated between making underground movies and European soft porn. Balch, a Burroughs fan, was interested in applying the cut-up to cinema. Later that year they began filming *Towers Open Fire* – a phrase taken from *Nova Express* – and used the Beat Hotel and the British Film Institute as a backdrop. Two more short films spilled over from the first – *The Cut Ups* and *Bill and Tony* – and all three were screened as part of the same package. With a cast consisting of Balch, Burroughs, Sommerville, Alexander Trocchi and Michael Portman, this piece of cinema proved to be one of those events that it is better to think about than to watch. There is no plot or dialogue, and the narrative consists of a series of jump cuts, superimposed images, repeated phrases and a distorted soundtrack. It is an all-out assault on the senses, almost defying the audience not to keep on watching. Like the cinema of Warhol, these films are works of defiant nonengagement – experiences that force the viewer to reconsider the extent of their commitment to the camera. Balch's work had its fifteen minutes of infamy on the alternative circuit, mainly on the crest of Burroughs's success, and now stands as little more than a curio of its times, a footnote reminding us that other people's egos can be as tedious as their dreams.

London, 1972.

Sommerville had now graduated, and he and Burroughs took a trip to Marrakesh before settling into a penthouse in the heart of Tangier. Burroughs had received a substantial cheque from Grove Press and contacted his parents with a view to establishing a trust fund for Billy Jnr. Instead it was decided that the son should go and stay with his father, who enrolled him in the American School at Tangier. The sixteen-year-old boy managed to last three days before dropping out. Far from resulting in bonding, the time spent together by father and son was forced and awkward, with the ghost of Joan haunting their strained silences. 'Off-key' was how Burroughs described it in his afterword to his son's novel, *Kentucky Ham*, 'the right thing said at the wrong time, the wrong thing said at the right time, and all too often, the wrongest thing said and done at the wrongest possible time'. Tangier itself had changed; the authorities were now trying to rid the city of its image as the paedophile capital of the world. 'What you see here is the Arabs at their worst,' wrote Burroughs to Gysin. 'No guts left in this miserable town.' In December 1963 he left for New York, joining Gysin who was trying to market his Dream Machine there. Sommerville failed to get a visa, and returned to England feeling rejected and bitter.

On his return to the States Burroughs was approached by *Playboy* to write a 'St Louis Return' piece – an article which, when written, they rejected. (It eventually surfaced in late 1965 in the *Paris Review*.) Burroughs would have to return to Palm Beach again in January 1965, this time to bury his father.

He spent until August 1965 in New York, staying first at the Chelsea Hotel and then in a loft on 210 Center Street. The notoriety around *The Naked Lunch* had made him the darling of the downtown artisans, and he contributed various cut-ups to the underground press as well as giving occasional performances to audiences that included Warhol and Diane Arbus. Gysin was receiving little interest in his Dream Machine, but an alternative creative outlet was his collaboration with Burroughs on the cut-ups that would later appear in *The Third Mind*. Yet although their attention flattered him, New York's literati stifled Burroughs. He wrote to Sommerville: 'I have missed you a great deal. Life in America is really a bore.' He returned to London in September 1965 and, after a brief trip to Tangier whilst his visa became legitimate, would settle there in 1966 for the next seven years.

Chapter 8

When Burroughs took up residence at 8 Duke Street, St James's, Ian Sommerville came with him. The problem was that Sommerville also brought with him his new boyfriend, Alan Watson. By agreeing to the arrangement Burroughs was knowingly entering an emotional minefield. As had happened with Ginsberg and Orlovsky, his emotional life was instantly fraught with rejection, jealousy and unrequited passion. An uneasy truce was gradually established, although Burroughs and Sommerville would never reclaim the intimacy they had once had.

Another domestic drama was playing itself out in Palm Beach, where the behaviour of his son was becoming more erratic and self-destructive. When still in high school he had got into the habit of forging prescriptions, and was lucky not to be expelled. On graduating, he took a speed-fuelled road trip to New York and found himself arrested twice in two weeks. Ginsberg bailed him out both times, but when he got busted again, in November of the same year, Burroughs was forced to return home and face his responsibilities. He arrived that Christmas to find his mother in the early stages of senile dementia and his son depressed and addicted. Burroughs himself was attempting to kick yet another habit and was having difficulty distinguishing his son's syringes from his own. Billy Jnr's lawyer plea-bargained a four-year

VALVULES
DE LA VEINE

probation on the condition that his client would take the cure. In February 1967 Burroughs took his son to the Lexington Clinic, and the story goes that when they arrived at the admissions desk the clerk looked at the pair and asked, 'Which one of you is checking in here?'

Back in London he began to pursue an almost obsessive interest in Scientology, a philosophy in which he had taken a passing interest since the early sixties. It may seem contradictory that a man so wary of thought-control should be drawn to Hubbard's pseudo-theology. Yet its attraction for Burroughs lay in the idea that followers could be deprogrammed – could be made aware of the knee-jerk responses into which we are conditioned. Early in 1967 he underwent the Joburg – a kind of spiritual polygraph that was designed to unmask beliefs so deeply ingrained that you were unaware of their presence. Burroughs has always claimed that this was purely experimental, although to Sommerville he seemed possessed by the monomania of a convert.

Movie parts and cameos started coming in. Left: A still and an off-screen shot from Conrad Rook's *Chappaqua*, 1967.

The Englishman moved out, but Burroughs continued to run audits on anyone who would listen, advertising free deconditioning sessions in the window of Barry Miles's Indica bookshop. Burroughs championed it as 'a real science of communication', explaining that 'they have a great deal of very precise data on words and the effects produced by words'. It is possible that he found in Scientology a theological equivalent of his own aesthetic endeavour – placing language under erasure and allowing the subject an insight into the way in which his mind has been scripted. At the same time, he was aware of the danger that the religion's promise of freedom could easily be read as an alternative prison. He mistrusted Hubbard and would later reflect that 'Scientology was useful to me until it became a religion and I have no use for religion. It's just another one of those control-addict trips and we can all do without those.'

ALLEN GINSBERG, WILLIAM BURROUGHS, JEAN GENET, RICHARD SEAVER (GROVE PRESS) AT THE DEMOCRATIC NATIONAL CONVENTION AUGUST 30, 1968

122

London was taking on some strange shapes, and it was with some relief that Burroughs accepted a commission from *Esquire* in August 1968 to cover the Democratic convention in Chicago. Of course the event and its attendant riots would be immortalized by Norman Mailer in his book *Miami and the Siege of Chicago*, but for Burroughs it was as much of an excuse to meet up with Jean Genet and Terry Southern, who were also covering it, as it was to witness the mechanisms of American politics. Although he marched on the Hilton (where he bumped into Ginsberg), Burroughs managed to side-step the brutality that Mailer recorded between the police and the protesters. 'Nothing surprised him favorably or unfavorably,' wrote Mailer, a statement that succinctly captured Burroughs's political disinterest. Indeed he spent most of his time holed up in the Hotel Delmonico, thinking up ways in which he and Genet could best utilize *Esquire*'s expense account, and playing host to the permanently pissed Jack Kerouac.

William Burroughs – an exile in Paris, a tourist in his own body. Left: Photographed here with Allen Ginsberg (left) and Jean Genet (right).

Though Burroughs may have had little interest in the politics of Chicago, the explosion of dissent that he witnessed there provided a catalyst for the action in *The Wild Boys* – the book he began writing in earnest on his return to London. Unlike his previous work, this novel does not have its origins either in notes that he had collected, or in any spill-over from his other novels. Started in 1967 and finished in August 1969, *The Wild Boys* signals an entirely new phase of literary productions – a move away from the cannibalistic world of cut-up, and towards a flourish for narrative and a return to routine. Character once more became a governing factor, with figures such as Audrey Carsons and the Frisco Kid looming as large in this text as Dr Benway had done in *The Naked Lunch*.

The novel envisions a world torn between the anarchic hedonism of its eponymous heroes and the frigid conformity of an establishment ruled by Colonel Greenfield. The wild boys are propelled by the forces of Eros and Thanatos, their demonic sexuality a celebration of appetites that society would prefer to ignore. Film is introduced as a controlling motif, suggesting that the reality of the scenes are to be located in our collective unconscious. There is another world, says the cinema, and it is the one we already inhabit. The occult constantly hovers beneath the book's surface, acknowledging the influence of the *Tibetan Book of the Dead*. The text moves between the utopia of sexual licence and the dsytopia of social control – as though the riots in Chicago had taken place outside a male brothel. As the wild boys' manifesto puts it:

We intend to march on the police machine everywhere....The family unit and its cancerous expansion into tribes, countries, nations we will eradicate at its vegetable roots. We don't want to hear any more family talk, mother talk, father talk, cop talk, priest talk, country talk, or party talk. To put it country simple we have heard enough bullshit.

The year the book was completed thousands of gay men, tired of police intimidation, would do battle with them on the streets of New York – an event that would come to be remembered as Stonewall. Grove Press published the book in 1971, although Burroughs had enough material left over for two more – *Exterminator!* and *Port of Saints*, both of which continue the wild boys' adventures.

Alongside this fiction Burroughs had been compiling a collection of essays and interviews with the French writer Daniel Odier. Originally conceived as being part of *The Wild Boys*, the collection (published as *The Job*) in effect works as the theoretical basis for his wild boy fantasies. Yet reading *The Job* alongside the three novels is not so simple an equation as theory and practice, journalism and fiction. Phrases recur, metaphors cross from one genre to the other, the dialogue of interview often mirrors the exchanges in the novels. In this sense Burroughs is one of the great unsung practitioners of 'faction' – the blending of fact and fiction, reality and fantasy, that suggests both the truth and the unreliability of either. Burroughs's work resists any neat categorization, or as he put it, 'All my books are one book. It's just a continuous book.' Earlier I claimed that Burroughs exists almost despite his texts, to which one could readily respond that he exists *only* within them. Both claims could be true, for as he remarked himself, 'Every word I write is autobiography. Every word is fiction.'

On 21 October 1969 Jack Kerouac's cirrhotic liver finally lost its battle with the booze.

With Sommerville gone, Burroughs found solace with a young Irishman called John Brady – one of Piccadilly's rent-boys, who drank too much and lied even more. It was a pale pastiche of his previous romance, since Brady had no interest in his writing or ideas and was constantly asking for financial 'incentives' to stick around. Not only that, but he was essentially a heterosexual who saw Burroughs purely as a meal ticket, and he would often bring women back to their apartment in Duke Street. Burroughs stayed with Brady out of a mixture of despair and self-loathing – feelings that were accentuated the longer he stayed with him.

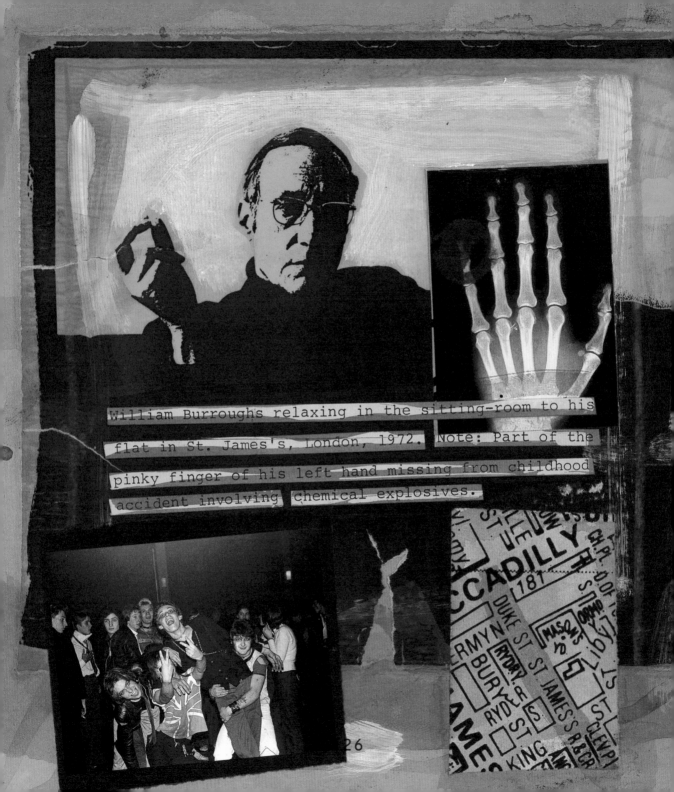

William Burroughs relaxing in the sitting-room to his flat in St. James's, London, 1972. Note: Part of the pinky finger of his left hand missing from childhood accident involving chemical explosives.

It was also a time of loss. On 21 October 1969 Jack Kerouac's cirrhotic liver finally lost its battle with the booze and drowned the forty-seven-year-old in his own blood. A year and a day later Burroughs's mother died in a nursing home, her mind having deserted her long before. Also in 1970 the poet Charles Olson died, aged sixty – a man who may not have been a close friend, but who represented a certain kind of avant-garde ambition. Burroughs's life at this time seems to be dominated by a sense of entropy – a fizzling out of possibilities, potential closing itself down. An abortive expedition to teach at an alternative college in Switzerland and a failed attempt to break into Hollywood with Terry Southern both added to the air of increasing ennui.

London became the focus of his frustration: he found in its pub hours and lack of pornography an expression of England's conservative parochiality. 'Never go too far in any direction is the basic rule on which Limey Land is built,' he wrote in *Exterminator!*, and would later tell a punk magazine that he sent 'a letter of support to the Sex Pistols when they released "God Save the Queen" in England because I've always said that the country doesn't stand a chance until you have 20,000 people saying BUGGER THE QUEEN! And I support the Sex Pistols because this is constructive, necessary criticism of a country which is bankrupt.'

In 1973 Ginsberg visited Burroughs and found him drunk and lethargic, his pallor as grey as the English weather. When he returned to New York he persuaded the City College to hire Burroughs to teach on their newly formed creative writing programme. For a fee of $7000 he was offered a three-month contract to begin the following year, the same month as his sixtieth birthday.

Left: Burroughs, London, 1972. 'Never go too far in any direction is the basic rule on which Limey Land is built,' he wrote in *Exterminator!*. 'BUGGER THE QUEEN! And I support the Sex Pistols.'

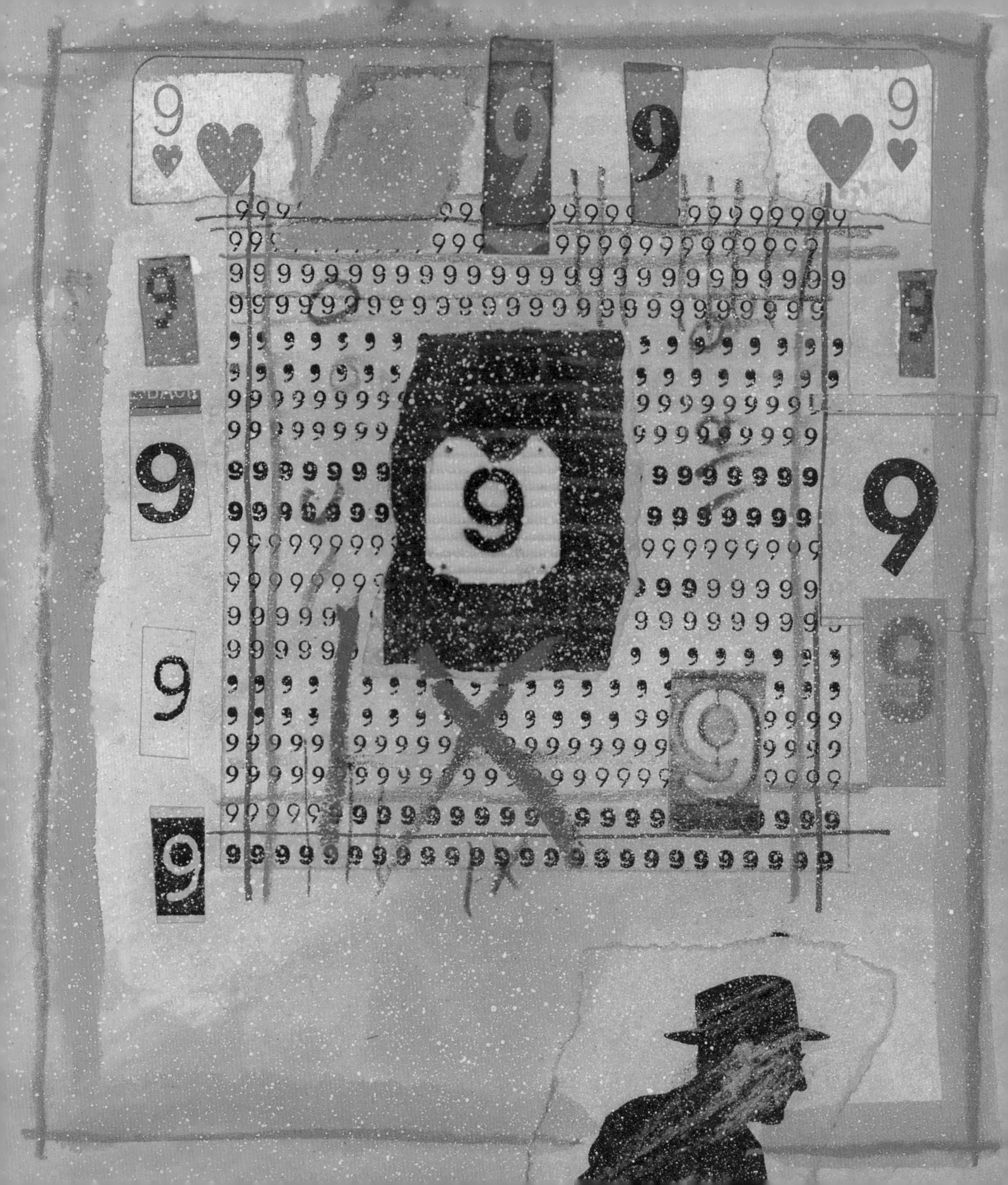

Chapter 9

After his drab confinement in London, New York unleashed a whole new Burroughs – extroverted, networked and productive. Through Ginsberg he met a fresh-faced Beat with an entrepreneurial flare named James Grauerholz. Born in Kansas, Grauerholz had made the exodus to New York, following the glory-trail of the Beats. He contacted Ginsberg, enclosing a photo of himself; after a brief fling their friendship soon flourished. It was Ginsberg who realized that Grauerholz's business acumen and energy could capitalize on Burroughs's reputation. Following a short affair Grauerholz became Burroughs's secretary, organizing readings and lectures that could command up to $1000 a time. In the young man Burroughs had found a soul-mate – a friend who had both enthusiasm for his work and practicality to make sure it got done. Grauerholz became the mainstay of his life until the end, running William Burroughs Communications from his base in Lawrence, Kansas.

It was through his time spent on the reading circuit that Burroughs cultivated himself as a performer. His gravelled drawl brought out the cynical humour of his routines – the blasphemous outrage of his material contrasting with the wry understatement of its delivery. His readings manage to be

both visceral and automated, as though he is ventriloquist and dummy in one. Listening to his 1970s' recordings now, one can envision his later incarnation as the junkie–priest in *Drugstore Cowboy*. His voice contains all the deranged tones of prophecy, yet there is a deadened flatness to it which refuses to be surprised by its own imaginings. It is the voice of a seance in reverse, hypnotized by its own mischievous alchemy.

While Burroughs was busy performing and writing a column for *Crawdaddy*, teaching creative writing seemed to prevent him from actually doing any. As he recalled, 'I also discovered that the image of "William Burroughs" in my students' minds had little relation to the facts. They were disappointed because I wore a coat and tie to class; they had expected me to appear stark naked with a strap-on, I presume. In all, a disheartening experience.' When his teaching job finished he settled his affairs in London and then returned to New York, eventually settling at 222 Bowery – an ex-YMCA that would become known as the Bunker.

It was here that *Cities of the Red Night* took its published form, although he had begun writing it on first returning to the States. The novel took nearly seven years to write and is really three books in one – a trio of narratives that draws on the genres of boys' adventure, science fiction and hard-boiled detective. It stands as the culmination of his earlier obsessions, and is arguably his most ambitious work since *The Naked Lunch*.

In moving from a pastiche of a pirate's tale through the virus of a futuristic dystopia to the me(a)n streets of urban mystery, *Cities of the Red Night* continues to map out his personal mythology. As in the *Nova* trilogy, characters from previous books reappear, phrases

Growing Up: CRAWDADDY

Exclusive Contributions by

JOHN LENNON, ERICA JONG, MUHAMMAD ALI

Studs Terkel, Souther, Hillman AND Furay, Steve Garvey,
Loudon Wainwright III, I.F. Stone, Rodney Dangerfield
and many, many more!

Led Zeppelin,
Jimmy Page & Rock Magic
by William Burroughs

almost never, and when it does it's worse th
foaling in the public street . . . trampled ruptur
heaps . . .
    "You know, Jimmy," I said: "The crowd
heavy piece of equipment falls on the crowd,
and then . . . a sound like falling mounta
CLICK CLICK: Jimmy Page did not bat
    "Yes, I've thought about that. We all h
thing is maintain a balance. The kids com
the music. It's our job to see they have a
trouble."
    And remember the rock group called Sto
hall in Switzerland . . . fire . . . exits loc
people dead including all the performers
who has never thought about fire and pa
The best way to keep something bad from
ahead of time, and you can't see it if
possibility. The bad vibes in that danc
really heavy. If the performers had be

ROCK MAGIC

By William Burroughs

Jimmy Page, Led Zeppelin, and A Search for the Elusive Stairway to Heaven

When I was first asked to write an article [on the] Led Zeppelin group, to be based on a [visit to] a concert and talking with Jimmy Page, [I was] not sure I could do it, not being suf[ficiently] knowledgeable about music to attemp[t any]thing in the way of musical criticism or even evalua[tion. I] decided simply to attend the concert and talk with Jimmy [Page,] and let the article develop. If you consider any set o[f data] without a preconceived viewpoint, then a viewpoint will e[merge] from the data.

My first impression was of the audience, as we stre[amed] through one security line after another—a river of y[oung people] looking curiously like a single organism: one well-beh[aved] clean-looking middle-class kid. The security guards seeme[d to] be cool and well-trained, ushering gate-crashers out wit[h a] minimum of fuss. We were channelled smoothly into our se[ats] in the thirteenth row. Over a relaxed dinner before the concert, [a] *Crawdaddy* companion had said he had a feeling that something bad could happen at this concert. I pointed out that [i]t always can when you get that many people together—like [b]ullfights where you buy a straw hat at the door to protect you [f]rom bottles and other missiles. I was displacing possible [d]anger to a Mexican border town where the matador barely es[c]aped with his life and several spectators were killed. It's known [a]s "clearing the path."

[Assu]mption of magic is the assertion of will as the prime[mover,] [mo]ving force in this universe—the deep conviction that nothing [ha]ppens unless somebody or some being wills it to happen. To [me] this has always seemed self-evident. A chair does not mov[e] [un]less someone moves it. Neither does your physical body, [w]hich is composed of much the same materials, move unless [y]ou will it to move. Walking across the room is a magical operation. From the viewpoint of magic, no death, no illness, no misfortune, accident, war, or riot is accidental. There are no accidents in the world of magic. And will is another word for animate energy. Rock stars are juggling fissionable material that could blow up at any time . . . "The soccer scores are coming in from the Capital . . . one must pretend an interest," drawled the dandified Commandante, safe in the pages of my book; and as another rock star said to me, "*You* sit on your ass writing—*I* could be torn to pieces by my fans, like Orpheus."

I found Jimmy Page equally aware of the risks involved in handling the fissionable material of the mass unconscious. I took on a valence I learned years ago from two *Life-Time* reporters—one keeps telling you these horrific stories: "Now old Burns was dragged out of the truck and skinned alive by the mob, and when we got there with the cameras the bloody thing was still squirming there like a worm . . ." while the other half of the team is snapping pictures CLICK CLICK CLICK to record your reactions—so over dinner at Mexican Gardens I told Jimmy the story of the big soccer riot in Lima, Peru in 1964.

We are ushered into the arena as VIP's, in the style made famous by *Triumph of the Will*. Martial [vi]stas—the statuesque police [crowd surging in a sultry [a]ir—grey clouds [last time . . .

. . . pieces—a policeman is [. . .] another hurled fifty feet down from the [. . . of] the stadium . . . bodies piled up ten feet deep at the exits. The soccer scores are coming in from the Capital . . . 306 . . . 318 . . . 352 . . . "I didn't know how bad it was until rain started to fall," said a survivor. You see, it never rains in Lima, or

William Burroughs is the author of Naked Lunch *and a dozen other novels, and is generally conceded to be one of the most significant American writers of this century. When Samuel Beckett was asked about Burroughs, he replied, "Well, he's a writer." Mr. Burroughs considers this a great compliment. He now resides in New York City.*

occur with a trance-like regularity, fact and fiction come together in order to fall apart. History dissolves into a perpetual present, driven by need, control and the need to control. It is a pioneering work of sublime post-modernity, a state perhaps best described by Don Delillo: 'Remarks existed in a state of permanent flotation. No one thing was either more or less plausible than any other thing. As people jolted out of reality, we were released from the need to distinguish.' Put another way, reading *Cities of the Red Night* is like experiencing *déjà vu* and amnesia at the same time.

Whilst Burroughs was working on this novel, New York was giving rise to other voices of urban disaffection – the confrontational indifference of punk. Based mainly around the St Mark's poetry and CBGB's club scenes, punk launched an assault on musical tradition in much the same way as Burroughs had done with literature. That self-styled Rimbaud of the stage, Patti Smith, may have announced that she didn't 'fuck much with the past but I've fucked plenty with the future', but the truth was that she achieved the latter precisely by fucking with the former. Smith's work embraced tradition with a snarling contempt, plundering her heritage with an anarchic abandon: 'in heart I am an American artist and I have no guilt. I seek pleasure. I seek the nerves under your skin.' Smith became a regular visitor to the Bunker: she and Burroughs found in each other a shared disrespect for the legacies they were reconstructing. To the punk-poetess, Burroughs was 'the father of heavy metal...who helped make the present possible by writing maps of territory that had previously been considered out of bounds', whilst he praised: 'The real impact of Patti Smith and the vitality that she produces in an audience and [her] whole electrical energy.'

Bands like The Ramones and The New York Dolls were presenting themselves as wilfully stupid, with 'vacant', 'dumb' and 'plastic' operating as their keywords. Yet such poses were not so much a revelation as an accusation – an attitude whose stubborn infantilism made a mockery of the world of maturity. It is no surprise that many punk artists found an affinity with Burroughs's work, both parties finding themselves imprisoned within forms through which they articulated their escape. Dissonance became pop music's cut-up, cover versions functioned as pastiche, the junkie became a figure of defiant oblivion. Victor Bockris's collection of interviews with Burroughs during his New York years features as many rock stars as writers – Debbie Harry and Lou Reed interspersed with Susan Sontag and Tennessee Williams. Having already been (illegitimately) adopted as the father of the Beats, Burroughs now had punk laying claim to him as its godfather. As Larry McCaffery has written:

Because his work has long been associated with graphic, wickedly humorous portrayals of drug addiction, violence, sexual perversion, and just about any other form of human depravity imaginable, Burroughs was quickly embraced by punk musicians as a fellow traveler in extremist aesthetics. Here was a figure whose very life was the embodiment of punk ideology, a man who had encouraged at least two generations of artists to boldly go to those forbidden areas of artistic expression where no artist had gone before. So it was during the mid-to-late 1970s that the Burroughs name...began appearing within the context of punk

Bands like The Ramones and The New York Dolls, Debbie Harry and Lou Reed launched an assault on musical tradition in much the same way as Burroughs had done with literature. Burroughs now had punk laying claim to him as its godfather.

138

mutations (New Wave, Industrial Noise and so on). Soon Burroughs became the equivalent of a rock star himself; songs were written about him, he was interviewed for major record magazines with Devo and other rock groups, he gave readings at rock concerts headlined by figures such as Jim Carroll and Patti Smith.

Burroughs at the Tropicana Hotel, Los Angeles, 1978. Photographed here with James Grauerholz (top left) and Christopher Isherwood, Bacardi, Leary, Bockris and Tynan (bottom left).

The image of Burroughs as proto-punk does not end with his impact on music. *Cities of the Red Night* was published in 1981, and it was only three years later that William Gibson produced the first of his cyberpunk novels, *Neuromancer*. Cyberpunk may now be firmly situated as an eighties' phenomenon – writing that captures both the fear and the fascination with new technology in all its forms, from the Walkman to Virtual Reality. It is a movement that addresses the frictional harmony between man and machine, a relationship that Bruce Sterling has characterized as 'pervasive, utterly intimate. Not outside us, but next to us. Under our skin; often inside our mind.' Yet retrospectively it is clear that Burroughs was writing cyberpunk before the term was invented, the *Nova* trilogy in particular meeting the concerns outlined by Sterling: 'The theme of body invasion....The even more powerful theme of mind invasion...techniques radically redefining the nature of humanity, the nature of the self.'

Placed in this context, Burroughs's work moves forward in history, finding itself echoed in the DIY bricolage of hip-hop, the fugitive manoeuvres of computer hacking, the disembodied androgyny of the Net. The Interzone of *The Naked Lunch* becomes John Shirley's Freezone – 'a city afloat in the wash of international confluence' – whilst hybrid realities surface as the favoured sites for Gibson's dystopias, areas where 'the street finds its own uses for things'. It is no coincidence that Ridley Scott looked to Burroughs for the title of his seminal cyber-film *Bladerunner* (a name Burroughs had in fact borrowed from Alan E. Nourse's book *The Blade Runner*). William Gibson has spoken of Burroughs's influence, saying:

> I'm of the first generation of American SF writers who had the chance to read Burroughs when we were fourteen or fifteen years old. I know having had that opportunity made a big difference in my outlook on what SF – or any literature, for that matter – could be. What Burroughs was doing with plot and language and other SF motifs I saw in other writers was literally mind-expanding. I saw this crazy outlaw character who seemed to have picked up SF and gone after society with it, the way some old guy might grab a rusty beer opener and start waving it around. Once you've had that experience, you're not quite the same.

Back in New York, Burroughs's life veered between lucrative celebrity and turbulent chaos. Being courted by rock stars had its downside, not least of which was that he felt obliged to befriend them. As Lou Reed once told Stewart Meyer, 'I'm surrounded by assholes. Even these people with me are assholes.' Punk's predilection for heroin was no secret and it was only a matter of time before Burroughs picked up their habits – just as they had picked up his.

On his sixty-second birthday Ian Sommerville sent him a telegram wishing him 'HAPPY BIRTHDAY. LOTS OF LOVE. LOTS OF PROMISE. NO REALIZATION.' Later the same day Anthony Balch sent him one – 'IAN SOMMERVILLE KILLED IN CAR ACCIDENT.' After

Ginsberg, Sommerville had been Burroughs's great love, and his death left a hole that he could fill only through drugs and heavy drinking. Four years later he would lose Balch to cancer.

Billy Jnr, meanwhile, was busy proving he was his father's son. After a failed marriage, two sub-Beat novels and an increasing dependence on alcohol, he received a stay of self-destruction by being given a teaching post in Naropa, Colorado, via some string-pulling by Ginsberg. But the reprieve did not last long, and in August 1976 he was admitted to Denver General where he lapsed into a six-day coma. His liver had given up the ghost and he was kept alive only by an artificial respirator. Denver General was, by remarkable coincidence, the only hospital in the country to perform liver transplants and, on his seventh day there, Burroughs Jnr was provided with a donor. The operation was a success for everyone except the patient, who found the prospect of being brought back to life more terrifying than the death that had awaited him.

In January 1977 he was discharged from hospital, armed with prescriptions for steroids and tranquillizers. But within a few months he had reintroduced booze into the cocktail and became a self-imposed vagrant. The poet Anne Waldman, who was a friend, recalls his 'haunting and harried presence as his condition worsened…Giving away money (his father had given him), befriending stray people, cats and dogs, collecting garbage (anything was salvageable)…wearing his heart and his wounds on his sleeve.'

During the next four years he assaulted his new liver with the same vehemence that had destroyed his own, and his life became one long forlorn journey between the hospitals, psychiatric institutes and halfway houses in Denver and Boulder. Burroughs, Grauerholz and Ginsberg made regular visits, although their attempts at support served only to inscribe him into his alienation. Billy Jnr simultaneously denounced his father yet craved his approval, forcing him into a testing game that neither could ever win. On 2 March 1981 he was found collapsed in a ditch by the side of a road in DeLand, Florida, and died in hospital early the next morning.

In many eyes Billy Jnr never stood a chance, possessing neither the talent nor the metabolism of his father and yet doomed to follow in his footsteps. As John Steinbeck Jnr, himself no stranger to the perils of parental infamy, wrote:

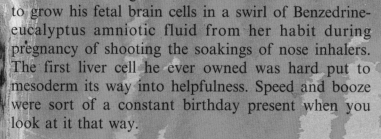

> Billy had a few strikes against him to be sure. He had tried to grow his fetal brain cells in a swirl of Benzedrine-eucalyptus amniotic fluid from her habit during pregnancy of shooting the soakings of nose inhalers. The first liver cell he ever owned was hard put to mesoderm its way into helpfulness. Speed and booze were sort of a constant birthday present when you look at it that way.

> Indeed, in one unsent letter to his father he had signed himself 'Your cursed from birth offspring', and he clearly felt that he had no choice but to play out a script that he had inherited rather than chosen.

Billy Jnr, 'Your cursed from birth offspring.'

Ginsberg took care of the funeral arrangements, opting for a Buddhist ceremony at the Rocky Mountain Dharma Center from which the ashes were scattered on 3 May. Burroughs remained in New York.

Cities of the Red Night was published the same year to largely hostile reviews, although this time the critics expressed boredom with his obsessions rather than shock. Thomas Disch in the *New York Times* was typical:

What Mr Burroughs offered the rubes [a term for bumpkins] back in 1959 and what he offers them today, in somewhat wearier condition, is entrance to a sideshow where they can view his curious id capering and making faces and confessing to bizarre inclinations. The backdrops are changed every few minutes by lazy stagehands, but the capering id delivers an identical performance before each one. It's grotesque, it's disgusting, but gosh – it's real! Readers who have never caught Mr Burroughs's act would do better to read *Naked Lunch* than this rather anemic clone.

In expanding the boundaries of the possibilities for fiction, Burroughs had managed the somewhat dubious achievement of making himself seem dated.

Next page. Photographs from the Nova Convention, 1978.

By March '79 James Grauerholz had moved back to Kansas, the emotional toll of Billy Jnr and the strain of managing Burroughs coalescing into New York burn-out. He delegated responsibility for Burroughs to the poet John Giorno, who lived in the same building. Despite Giorno's efforts, when Grauerholz returned to New York in June 1980 he found a hospital-thin Burroughs who was back living on junk-time. But Grauerholz had problems of his own back in Kansas and returned there, leaving Burroughs to fend for himself. The rock star circus continued with Giorno, Burroughs and Victor Bockris playing host to David Bowie, Joe Strummer and the Rolling Stones. Warhol was also an occasional visitor, and the conversations that Bockris recorded between the strung-out writer and the terminally blank artist are masterpieces of hypnotic vacuity. In fact Bockris's 'Report from the Bunker' can be viewed as a document of disintegration, a reminder that the figure of the addict may be glamorous to look at, but deathly to listen to.

NOVA 1978

WILLIAM BURROUGHS AND FRANK ZAPPA AT THE NOVA CONVENTION · 1978 MARCIA RESNICK

BRION GYSIN AND WILLIAM BURROUGHS AT THE NOVA CONVENTION #1 1978 MARCIA RESNICK

144 AT THE NOVA CONVENTION 1978
GIORNO, GYSIN, R·RICARD,

ALLEN GINSBERG, TERRY SOUTHERN & WILLIAM BURROUGHS AT NOVA CONVENTION · 1978 · N.Y.C.   MARCIA RESNICK

145   MARCIA RESNICK

BURROUGHS, BOCKRIS, DAVID YOUNG AND UNKNOWN EXTRA PERSON

In September 1980 Burroughs took a methadone cure at Dr Karkus's clinic at 27 East 92nd Street – an out-patient programme designed to leave him clean within a couple of weeks. Having completed his treatment, Burroughs gave a reading in Lawrence, Kansas that had been arranged by Grauerholz, writing to Gysin: 'that place in Kansas could be a nice spot for old age, feeding your goldfish in the evening in the garden pool'. He wasn't joking. Lawrence was a small university town and provided a comforting contrast to the hustle and heroin of New York. The decision was almost made for him when he returned to the Bowery to find that his rent had increased from $355 to $710 per month. 'It simply isn't worth paying double to be in NYC,' he wrote to Gysin. 'So I found a place that is cheap, comfortable, and where I can work.'

Lawrence was a small university town and provided a comforting contrast to the hustle and heroin of New York.
'That place in Kansas could be a nice spot for old age,' Burroughs observed.

9 NINE → 10

From the
Bunker
Burroughs
played host
to popular
culture's
glitterati:
Bockris,
Anderson,
Giorno,
Warhol,
Jagger, to
name but
a few.

LAURIE ANDERSON, the New York-based performance artist who recently signed a major contract with Warner Bros. Records, appeared in concert at the Ritz on Sunday with the poet John Giorno and the author William Burroughs. The concert coincided with the release of an album featuring these three artists, who all share an oracular style of language, a fascination with technology, and an apocalyptic sensibility.

WILLIAM BURROUGHS, LAURIE ANDERSON AND JOHN GIORNO   1981   MARCIA RESNICK

MICK

ANDY

MARCIA RESNICK 1985

Chapter 10

To many of his friends, Giorno and Ginsberg especially, Burroughs's move to Kansas was his bid for splendid isolation. The prairies of the Midwest offered a kind of internal exile, an all-American equivalent of the distance he had sought in Tangier, Paris or London. Yet it was after this move that the Burroughs myth proliferated, resurfacing in advertising, movies and music. It was as though the vacuum left by his person was filled by his much larger persona – 'Burroughsian' became a synonym for the experimental, the excessive, the dangerous. From his base in Kansas Burroughs had discovered that most paradoxical form of privacy – the art of hiding in plain sight. His public self became an open book, the text that is the most difficult to read.

MODEL HOME IN MORE WAYS THAN ONE

With characteristic perversity, the nomadic Burroughs bought a one-storey, white-painted wood-frame house on Learnard Street for $36,000. At the age of nearly seventy, he became a first-time buyer. Though the cost of living was less, money continued to be a problem, and he had no sooner set up home than he was forced to go on a reading tour to keep up with the mortgage and the rent for the office of Burroughs Communications. It was not until 1984 that he became financially stable when his new agent, Andrew Wylie, would secure him the kind of deal that made Martin Amis the envy of literary London.

As Burroughs moved west, so did his fiction. *The Place of Dead Roads*, the second book of the *Cities* trilogy, was begun in Boulder in around 1978 but only written in earnest once he was ensconced in Kansas. Its narrative moves from the turn of the century to the present, and hinges on the exploits of an archetypical gunslinger, Kim Carsons – 'a slimy, morbid youth of unwholesome proclivities with an insatiable appetite for the extreme and the sensational'. Burroughs appropriates the pulp Western genre to explore the possibilities of time travel – a combination which suggests that the astronaut is a mythical descendant of the gunman. Whether it be the space race or the Wild West, the idea of a frontier becomes a key metaphor for the American psyche – a place whose barren absence generates the necessity for self-reliance and rampant individualism. Burroughs parodies the notion of virgin soil, replacing it instead with one of amoral neutrality. Carsons is not a man with an eye for natural justice, but a force for the unfettered libido, a libertine on horseback. Into a genre well known for its heterosexual swagger Burroughs injects an orgiastic series of homosexual encounters – as though Clint Eastwood had been recast in a leather bar.

Dead Roads was published in February 1984 to lukewarm reviews. The *New York Times* complained that, 'There are so many nearly identical couplings and killings, that more than once I thought I'd lost my page and read the same passage over again.'

That reviewer may be right – the only problem being that he writes as though this is a bad thing. For the novel is precisely about the instability of history – an unreliable past making unexpected appearances in an uncertain present. Or as Burroughs succinctly put it, 'My hero, Kim Carsons, begins tampering with the prerecordings. In other words, he cuts in on God's monopoly. And that's one of the things the book's about, and how he is able to move about backwards and forwards in time.'

The overspill from *Dead Roads* formed the basis for the final book of the trilogy, *The Western Lands* – a work that was begun in 1983 and would take four years to complete. It is reflective in tone and more conventional in form, and Burroughs looked to the world of ancient Egypt as a place where he could muse on the nature of immortality, sorcery, appetite and space. The book occupies – or is occupied by – a parallel universe, one in which secrets are social, not private, and in which mysticism is a foundation for history rather than a retreat from it. 'I venture to suggest that at some time and place the animal Gods actually existed,' writes Burroughs,

and that their existence gave rise to belief in them. At this point the monolithic One God concept set out to crush a biologic revolution that could have broken down the lines established between the species, thus precipitating unimaginable chaos, horror, joy and terror, unknown fears and ecstasies, wild vertigos of extreme experience, immeasurable gain and loss, hideous dead ends.

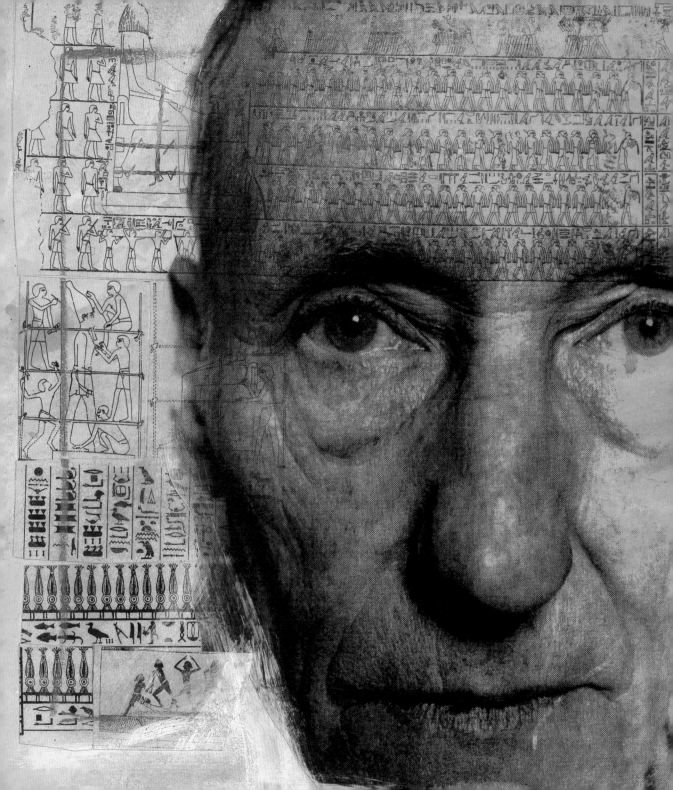

Put another way, the novel is not so much a work of magic realism as a study of the reality of magic. Like Mailer's *Ancient Evenings* – a book to which Burroughs acknowledges his debt – *The Western Lands* employs a radical nostalgia, a gaze that pierces our ideas of 'continuity' and 'development' and reminds us that 'all the filth and horror, fear, hate, disease and death of human history flows between you and the Western Lands'. We do not emerge victorious from the past, but labour slavishly beneath it. If this is nostalgia, Burroughs implies, then it certainly never was what it used to be.

For a writer so mistrustful of language, Egyptology provided a comfortable environment: its hieroglyphs offered a promise of contamination-free communication, a space in which signifier and signified could co-habit without the threat of infection. Then again, Burroughs is writing about hieroglyphics and is not their practitioner, and his book ends with the death-rattle of its own design: 'The old writer couldn't write anymore because he had reached the end of words, the end of what can be done with words.' Burroughs did in fact continue to write and publish, but this sense of finality signals an exhaustion with fiction, a Beckettian weariness whereby he can't go on; and yet he did go on. The books that materialized subsequently have none of the immediacy, scale or engagement of their predecessors. Whereas *The Naked Lunch* or the *Nova* trilogy were attempts to intervene in the possibilities of writing, a work like *My Education: A Book of Dreams* is a notebook which speculates on the sources of that intervention. It is a book of retroactive interest, a map of an inner life whose contours have already been outlined. Reading *A Book of Dreams* to find out about Burroughs's

Egyptology attracted Burroughs to hieroglyphs as a virus-free language.

unconscious would be like reading *Jokes and Their Relation to the Unconscious* to discover Freud's sense of humour.

After *The Western Lands* the image of Burroughs as the pioneer of American Literature is replaced with that of the Man with Nothing to Prove. Being Burroughs became an occupation in itself, as though he were the old guard and the avant-garde rolled into one; our only expectations being that he would continue to defy them.

The funereal quality of *The Western Lands* was not just a literary motif; death, it seemed, was surrounding Burroughs throughout its composition. No sooner had he settled in Lawrence in 1983 than his brother Mort died at the age of seventy-three. Burroughs returned to St Louis for the funeral, the last of his dwindling clan. Later the same year he lost Tennessee Williams, a writer with whom he had developed a strong rapport during his time in the Bunker. Ironically, one of their favoured topics of discussion had been the nature of death, with Williams confessing how he had 'always been terrified of' it and trying to figure out ways by which he could 'postpone the event'. Burroughs would turn the problem on its head, replying that 'One of my students once asked me if I believed in the afterlife and I said, "How do you know you're not already dead?"' In April 1986 Jean Genet died, taking with him the archetype for the writer-as-outlaw. Burroughs inherited the title.

Brion Gysin's health was also rapidly deteriorating. He had already undergone a colostomy and was suffering from emphysema, and now his doctors diagnosed him as having lung cancer. Burroughs and Grauerholz made several trips to Paris to visit him, and the antiseptic horror of their friend's condition bursts through *The Western Lands*: 'Cancer wards where death is as banal as a bedpan. Just an empty bed to prepare for the next Remains. The walking Remains, who fill up the vast medical complexes, haunted by nothingness.' On 13 July 1986, Gysin's nurse arrived at his hotel to find him dead of a heart-attack. He was seventy years old.

Whereas many of his contemporaries became icons through their death, Burroughs seems to have become one through defying it. In an America busy waging war on drugs, Burroughs refused to be a casualty. The very act of staying alive, of being stubbornly unrepentant, became a way of talking back to the Surgeon General's moral panic. 'Why do you think they call it dope?' asks the anti-drugs commercial. In the persona of Burroughs the media received an unsolicited reply, a response that made their rhetorical question sound more vacuous than the object of its cheap derision. This is not to claim that Burroughs was a testament to the benefits of drugs, but rather that he upset the simplistic equations of addiction and morality, illness and decline.

Whilst he was completing the trilogy, *Queer* was eventually published, a mere thirty years after it had been written. This time Bill Lee substitutes junk for booze, cruising the bars of Mexico in search of intimacies with strangers. Pitched somewhere between Joe Orton and Bukowski, Lee's encounters stagger from commercial transactions with rent-boys to the stilted comforts of an ex-GI named Allerton. The novel evokes a kind of frigid eroticism, an anti-pornography that is ashamed of its own sexual *frisson*. In the introduction Burroughs draws out the distinction between his first novel and its sequel: 'In my first novel, *Junkie*, the protagonist "Lee" comes across as integrated and self-contained....In *Queer* he is

WILLIAM [...] [...]
70th BIRTHDAY,
NEW YORK, 1984
copyright 1991 KATE SIMON

William S. Burroughs
on his 70th Birthday,
Left to Right:
John Giorno, Jim Carroll,
Bill Burroughs, Lydia Lunch,
David Johansen.

Bill Burroughs 70th Birthday

Left to right: John Giorno, Jim Carroll, Bill[...]
Lydia Lunch, Da[...]

I AM SEVENTY

disintegrated, desperately in need of contact, completely unsure of himself and of his purpose.' The novel, in this sense, is less about the presence of sex and more about the absence of junk. On drugs Lee is purely inner-directed, needing nothing but the needle to keep him cocooned in the self. Without them his identity can only be negotiated through the Other, his lovers acting as mirrors to remind him of who he is. Hell is other people, remarked Sartre. *Queer* goes one further, suggesting that hell is our need for other people.

'At the beginning of the *Queer* manuscript fragment,' writes Burroughs,

Lee seems determined to score, in the sexual sense of the word. There is something curiously systematic and unsexual about his quest for a suitable sex object, crossing one prospect after another off a list which seems compiled with ultimate failure in mind. On some deep level he does not want to succeed, but will go to any length to avoid the realization that he is not really looking for sex contact.

What Burroughs is pinpointing is the claustrophobia of having every fibre of his being tied up with his sexuality – the artificiality of a gay identity, what Foucault called a 'hermaphrodization of the soul'. The irony of Burroughs's title is that for him homosexuality is a performance and not a definition; 'queer' functions as an adjective rather than as a noun.

Vladimir Nabokov famously attributed the inspiration for *Lolita* to a story about a gorilla in captivity who produced the first drawing by an animal – 'sketch [which] showed the bars of the poor creature's cage'. And like literature's most infamous pederast, Lee too uses language to articulate the structure of his own imprisoning desire: 'Lee did not enjoy frustration. The limitations of his desires were like the bars of a cage, like a chain and collar, something he had learned as an animal learns, through days and years of experiencing the snubs of the chain, the unyielding bars.' Such imagery could not be further from the battle-cries of the post-Pill sexual freedom fighters. Our bodies are never ourselves, implies Burroughs – the two are too often in dispute. Sexual desire is not just a site for celebration, but an occasion for enslavement, a place where obsession and possession conspire to rob the individual of his autonomy.

It may be this suspicion of desire's duplicitous nature that has prevented Burroughs from being claimed by the growing ranks of gay critics and queer activists. Whilst their aim has been to reappropriate negative stereotypes, Burroughs appears to have taken a perverse delight in perpetuating them. The rhetoric of 'out and proud' empowerment does not sit easily on the shoulders of a man who wrote of his 'Curse...the painted, simpering female impersonators I had seen in a Baltimore night club. Could it be possible that I was one of those subhuman things?' Nor do the claims for same-sex attraction as being transgressive and dissident find much support in a writer who dismissed his sexuality as mere narcissism: '"They have maleness, of course. So have I. I want myself the same way I want others. I'm disembodied. I can't use my own body for some reason."' Queer nation's chant that 'We're Here, We're Queer, Get Used To It' is met by Burroughs's dispassionate ennui. We may be here and queer, he seems to be saying, but we're always going to be used by it. Burroughs may well be one of America's greatest homosexual writers. But he is certainly one of its most satirical homophobes.

Fortunately, Burroughs was never a writer to concern himself with the politics of the superego – the representations of what should be, rather than what is or could be. Experimentation was always his touchstone, the transgression of boundaries regardless of the social moralities contained therein. Burroughs may seem to have positioned himself within misogyny, homophobia or misanthropy, but his work relocates him into an aesthetic space whose only prejudice is against the limits of received convention.

If Burroughs's retirement to Kansas brought with it the winding down of his writing – his trilogy being a fiction which dug its own grave – it also catalysed his interest in new forms of expression. If the hieroglyph represented the golden age of the word, it also provides an occasion in which representation and referent are locked in symbiotic harmony. In short, the hieroglyph relocates the written word as an image, and this shift from the literary to the visual is one that Burroughs mirrored in his own production.

Late in 1982 Burroughs was engaged in his favourite pastime, shooting practice, when he 'picked up a piece of plywood and blasted it. Then I looked at the broken plywood where the shots came out and in these striations I saw all sorts of things – little villages, streets of all kinds. I said "My God, this is a work of art."' Just as cut-up had attempted to rub out the word, so his 'shotgun art' assaulted the canvas, an analogy that he had drawn on years earlier in 'Minutes to go': 'The cut-up method treats words as the painter treats his paint, raw materials with rules and reasons of its own.'

Burroughs may have chanced upon this form, although he remained aware that it was not without its precedents. The French artist Yves Klein had attacked his paintings with explosives in the

Burroughs, Jean-Michel Basquiat and
Debbie Harry, Christmas 1986.

late 1950s, whilst in the early 1960s Niki de Saint Phalle's *Tir* series had taken Jasper Johns's and Rauschenberg's assemblage paintings and shot at them with a .22 calibre rifle. Joe Goode had blasted his paintings, as had the American artist David Bradshaw who celebrated the act as 'an energy release with a finite point of focus'.

In an essay in *The Adding Machine*, Burroughs had posed the following question:

> If art has undergone such drastic alteration in the past hundred years, what do you think artists will be doing in fifty or a hundred years from now? Of course we can foresee expansion into the realm of exploding art....A self-destroying TV set, refrigerator, washing-machine, and electric stove going off, leaving a shambles of a gleaming modern apartment....What has happened here? Art has become literal and returned to its magical function of making it happen....Now suddenly art makes its lethal eruption into the so-called real world.

163

It is almost impossible for us not to play the armchair shrink, and regard Burroughs's paintings as an exorcism of the Ugly Spirit who had got in on the William Tell act that had ended Joan's life.

Yet they also belong in his artistic project, an attempt to integrate cohesion with contingency, the random with the specific, the violent with the sublime. Chance itself may be infinite, but the canvas is always finite, so that each of his paintings reminds us of what they could have been as well as what they are. The power of accident is both contained and unleashed, freeze-framing a moment whose composure is at odds with its composition. Burroughs savours the dangers of such tension, writing that 'I want my painting to literally walk off the goddamned canvas, to become a creature and a very dangerous creature. I see painting as evocative magic. And there must always be a random factor in magic, one which must be constantly changed and renewed.'

Burroughs held his first exhibition at the Tony Shafrazi Gallery in New York at the end of 1987. It sold out almost instantly, as did subsequent exhibitions at London's October Gallery, Vancouver's Front Gallery and the Casa Sin Nombre Gallery in Santa Fe. By 1989 Burroughs's paintings were commanding up to $3000 each, prompting their creator to remark, 'Painting is a lot easier than writing. A painting can take as little as twenty minutes, where a novel might take a year or more. I'm as deeply into painting as writing now; it occupies practically all my time.'

Or at least twenty minutes of his time. Not that we can accuse Burroughs of disingenuity or con-artistry, any more than one could 'accuse' Warhol of being fake or Jeff Koons of being kitsch. What is interesting about Burroughs's canvases is that they are canvases made by Burroughs – his signature inscribing them within the cross-

'A painting can take as little as twenty minutes, where a novel might take a year or more. I'm as deeply into painting as writing now; it occupies practically all my time.'

Floating some paintings to shoot, Feb, 1994

*William Burroughs gesturing over one of his pai*166

With painting

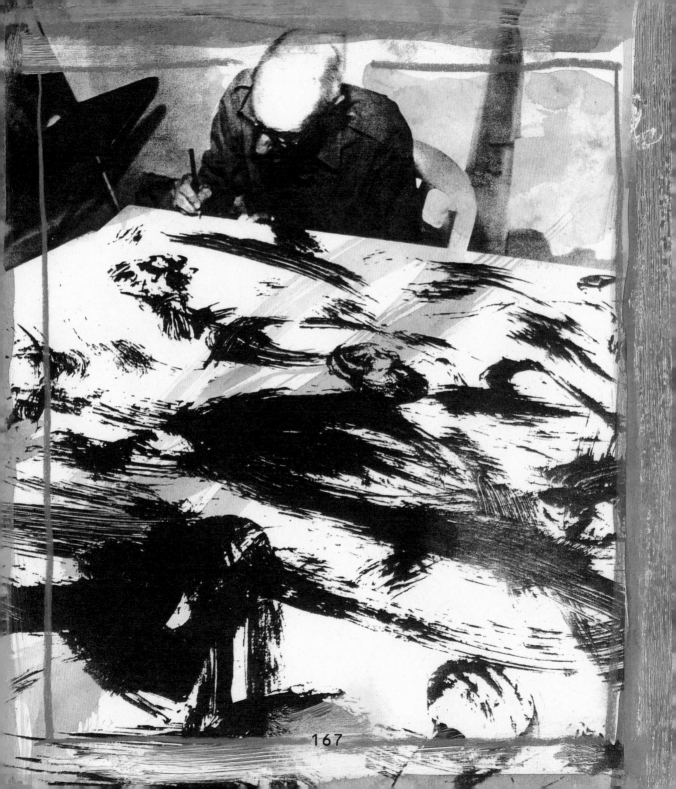

JACKSON
POLLOCK

Is he the greatest . . . living painter in the United States?

Recently a formidably high-brow New York critic hailed the brooding, puzzled-looking man shown above as a major artist of our time and a fine candidate to become "the greatest American painter of the 20th Century." Others believe that Jackson Pollock produces nothing more than interesting, if inexplicable, decorations. Still others condemn his pictures as degenerate and find them as unpalatable as yesterday's macaroni. Even in Pollock, at the age of 37, has burst forth as the shining new phenomenon of American art.

Pollock was virtually unknown in 1944. Now his paintings hang in five U.S. museums and 50 private collections. Exhibiting in New York last winter, he sold 12 out of 18 pictures. Moreover his work has stirred up a fuss in Italy, and distortions he is about. For a moment three intermittent people Paris—where he is fast becoming the most talked-of and most-argued U.S. painter. He has also won a following among his own neighbors in the village of Springs, N.Y., who answer themselves by trying to decide what his paintings are about. His prayer brought our subtly the identification for his filtered curving sameness in one case of view of Siberia. For Pollock's own explanation of why he paints as he does, turn the page.

fire of his own iconography. In place of the *objet trouvé* he offers us the *objet fusillé* – a shotgun relic that possesses the same schizophrenic charm as an autograph.

In a statement written for an exhibition in Rome, Burroughs acknowledged that his art's appeal always resides elsewhere, that the real action always takes place, as it were, off-stage:

> Norman Mailer kindly said of me that I may be 'possessed by genius'. Not that I am a genius, or that I possess genius, but that I may be at times, possessed by genius. I define 'genius' as the nagual, the unpredictable, the uncontrollable, spontaneous, alive, capricious and arbitrary. An artist is possessed by genius sometimes, when he is so lucky.

Burroughs replaces the clichéd question of 'Is it art?' with the more acute problem of 'Where is art?' Neither the property of an omniscient creator, nor the inherent meaning of an autonomous text, Burroughs's paintings seem to exist at the point where he is uncertain whether they exist at all:

> My painting derives from an innate disability. I cannot draw. Not a chair, not a table, not a tree. Consequently when I apply paint to a surface I do not know what will emerge....Clear recognizable images and scenes do emerge, but not through my conscious control. I quote from Wheeler's Recognition Physics: 'Nothing existsuntil it is observed.'

The art historian Robert A. Sobieszek has made the case for situating Burroughs primarily within the visual arts, arguing that his fold-ins and cut-ups are as much of a challenge to the pictorial as they are to the literary. In *Ports of Entry* he places Burroughs in a lineage that stretches from Jackson Pollock to Jean-Michel Basquiat:

The art historian Robert A. Sobieszek places Burroughs in a lineage that stretches from Jackson Pollock to Jean-Michel Basquiat.

Like viruses infinitely replicating themselves, Burroughs's chance operations are discovered in everything he does....His art is best characterized as a kind of expressive automatism wherein calligraphic gestures are merged with experimental effects in the production of meditative, surrealist *terrain vagues* or mindscapes. His style adopts many of the techniques and concepts of the earlier abstract art while casually insisting on an immaterial world of free-floating existence.

Certainly it is true that Burroughs could be taught within art history just as readily as he could within literary studies. Yet it is also true that both disciplines remain puzzled about what he is doing there.

Of all the critics, David Avery made the point most succinctly in his review of an exhibition held at the Los Angeles County Museum of Art:

William S. Burroughs' exhibit at LACMA has come under much scrutiny since its opening. Can someone who is primarily a writer paint with validity? Does the written word translate to the canvas? Is it art?

Definitions such as this are exactly what the work of Burroughs over the last forty years has been trying to abolish. His work...has always been an attempt to destroy the conventions of not only society, but of language and rational thought itself....Burroughs' goal has been to achieve a state of total freedom through the absence or anulment of linear logic, 'either-or-thinking'.

But is it art?

The only answer applicable is 'who cares?'

JESS STOCKSTILL
SHOOTERS SUPPLY
2536
GRA

UNTITLED
1992 →

Maybe the one person who would really have cared was Brion Gysin – a figure who had always felt that his artistic innovations had been conspiratorially ignored by an imagined coterie of matriarchs and heterosexists (a paranoia not necessarily ungrounded). Despite Burroughs's generous acknowledgements of his influence, Gysin remained convinced that he was seen as an acolyte to the junkie priest. Burroughs may have told Kathy Acker that it was Gysin who 'taught me how to see a picture', yet it is significant that he waited until after his friend's death to mount his first exhibition. As he confessed to Miles: 'I didn't start doing paper until after Brion's death, it would have been unthinkable for me to compete with him. I've done a lot better than he did, financially, on painting. Collaborating was one thing but as soon as I started painting that would be a matter of competition. Without question Brion would have seen it like that.'

Left: Untitled, 1992. Ready-made of hat, glasses, pistol holster and vodka bottle.
Like some pact between Narcissus and Midas, everything that Burroughs touched turned into himself.

It is but one more paradox that the phrase 'unique talent' should so consistently be applied to a man whose work has relied on collaboration. In his work with other artists, we never lose sight of the 'Burroughs-ness' of the project in question. His individuality is never diluted through the other, but rather enhanced by it – as though their presence is almost incidental to, or subsumed by, those ever-elusive narratives that lurk within him. His is a myth of omniscience whereby the people he works *with* end up working *for* the myth that the man embodies.

Like some pact between Narcissus and Midas, everything that Burroughs touched turned into himself. It made him as much of a virus as the language that he saw contaminating us.

11 →

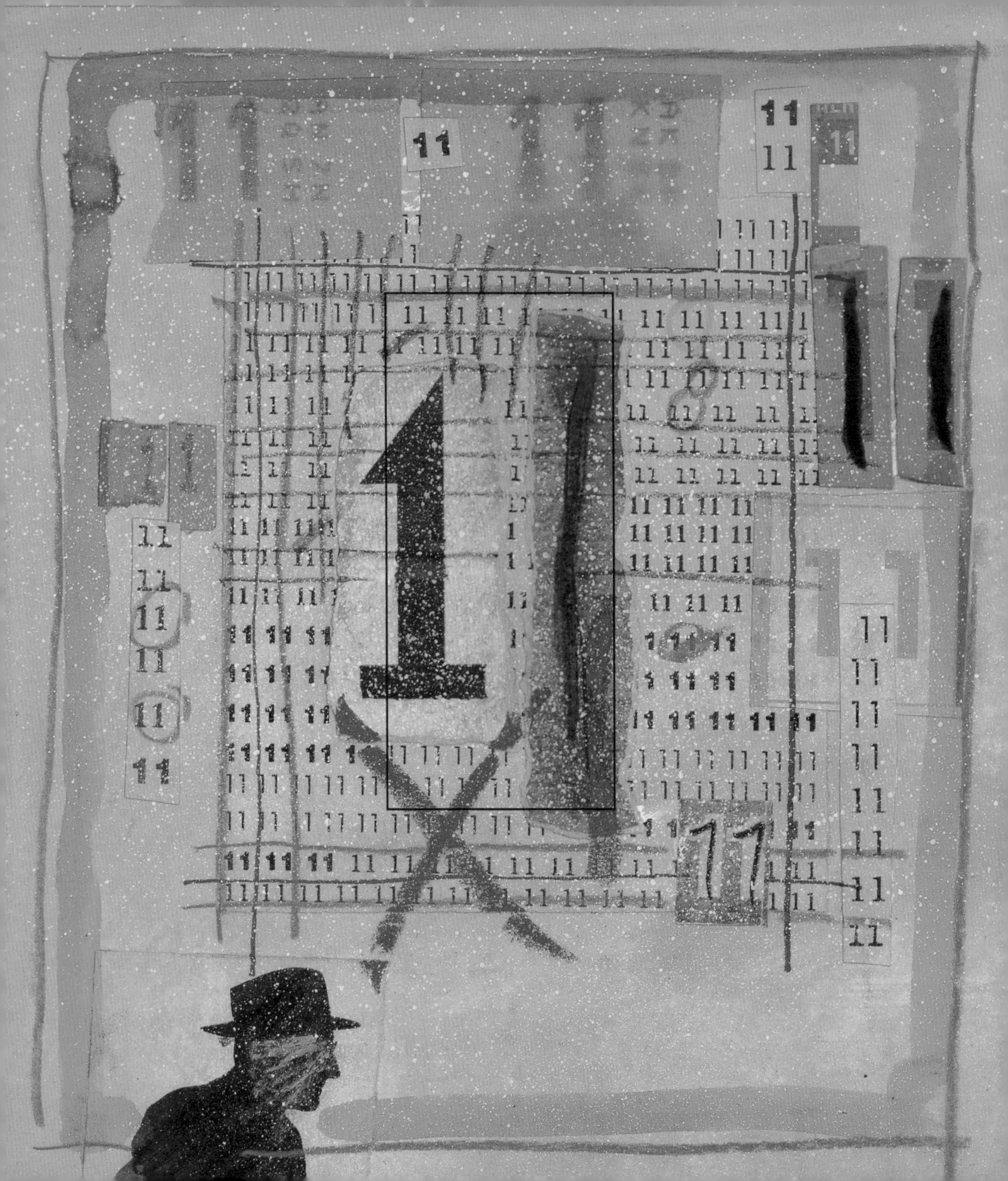

Chapter 11

Burroughs's ability to leave his iconic imprint on a collaborative medium has made him an ideal candidate for movie cameos. Michael Almereyda suitably typecast him as a gun freak in his 1989 black comedy *Twister*, whilst Jacob Burckhardt's *It Don't Pay to Be an Honest Citizen* saw him as a Mafia boss.

Of course, Burroughs's most memorable role was as Father Murphy, the junkie priest, in Gus Van Sant's 1989 film *Drugstore Cowboy*. Van Sant was a Burroughs fan of long standing, and, indeed, had based his student film *The Discipline of D.E.* on a short story by him. The film was to be set in Portland, Oregon, and it was here that the two men met to discuss the project. Burroughs had already written a piece entitled 'The "Priest", They Called Him', and this was to form the basis for his character. Van Sant was unhappy with his own dialogue, eventually relying on Grauerholz and Burroughs to provide their own spin for his character. 'I rewrote four scenes for William,' recalled Grauerholz, 'and then William put his own unique polish on it, his own imprimaturs.'

Burroughs's most
memorable role
was as Father
Murphy, the
junkie priest, in
Drugstore Cowboy
with Matt Dillon.

The result was a drug-fuelled road movie, with Matt Dillon and his gang dividing their time between raiding the chemists and getting strung-out in motel rooms. Its tone steered clear of being either overly romantic or morally judgemental, capturing instead both the squalor and excitement, the desperation and the liberation of the drifter in search of a fix. Van Sant cleverly captures the ambiguity of the American road – a place of flight as well as of freedom, a site in which mobility is enforced as much as it is chosen. Following Burroughs's dictum that 'Junk isn't a kick. It's a way of life', the film suggests how the gang are as addicted to robbing pharmacies as they are to their spoils, and that their evasion of the police gives them a high equal to that provided by the heroin. It is when the Dillon character decides to take the cure that he renews his friendship with Father Murphy, the now defrocked priest who years before turned him on to drugs.

In an otherwise positive review, Pauline Kael voiced the following misgiving:

> But the film errs, I think, in casting William S. Burroughs as the junkie priest. Dillon is acting, and Burroughs isn't, quite. He does have a performer's booming voice, and he stylizes his big line about narcotics having been 'systematically scapegoated and demonized'. But elsewhere the movie undercuts its characters' bravado, even as we're amused by it; it doesn't undercut him, and his scenes are too much of a guest-hipster number.

179

The key word here is 'quite' in the second sentence, for it suggests an alternative reading in which Burroughs is always acting, in which his very presence is always a performance. Not that there is a 'real' Burroughs against which we can judge a false one, but his status denies any distinction between the two. In the figure of Father Murphy he embodies many of the roles of his own mythology – the ruined paternalist, the irreligious prophet, the unrepentant addict, the undutiful father. Burroughs may appear to be not quite acting because his cameo has had the chance to be so well rehearsed. Burroughs is not so much playing himself as playing his selves – acting out the fictions of what has become his own character. Critics may not rate his ability to act, and yet there is another sense in which he is unable to do anything but.

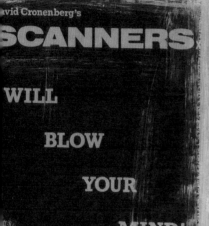

Films such as David Cronenberg's *Videodrome, Scanners* and *Dead Ringers* were Burroughs-infested studies in body-horror and physical mutation.

Burroughs did not have a cameo in *Drugstore Cowboy*, but the film did have a walk-on part in Burroughs's canon of iconography.

In 1981 the film-maker David Cronenberg told *Omni* magazine: 'Some part of me would love to make a movie of William S. Burroughs's *Naked Lunch*.' Although it would be nearly a decade before he actually did so, in one sense he already had. Films such as *Videodrome, Scanners* and *Dead Ringers* were Burroughs-infested studies in body-horror. Physical mutation, technological invasion, addiction, disgust and a visceral fascination underscored his movies just as they had driven Burroughs's writing. Cronenberg has frequently acknowledged the influence, claiming that it stifled him as a writer and yet set him free as a director:

When I did write, I was possessed by Nabokov and Burroughs. One of the things I had trouble with as a writer was getting out of their clutches. I couldn't find my own voice. But when I wrote for film, I was totally liberated....What I do is very different from Burroughs. There are influences and there are connections. One of the reasons you find a writer so compelling is that they crystallize for you stuff that's in you already. Images of addiction and body-consciousness, say....Mine? Well, it was there in Burroughs. Not all of it. Not all of it in Burroughs, and not all of it in me. But so much of it, right there, stuff I could have written, except Burroughs had been doing it so much better and for so much longer.

Although Cronenberg's was not the first bid to 'film the unfilmable' – Anthony Balch, Terry Southern and even Brion Gysin had each toyed with the idea – his was the one that seemed the most apposite. The two men had met at Burroughs's seventieth birthday party in New York, and in January 1985 Burroughs had, along with Cronenberg, Grauerholz, Jeremy Thomas and Hercules Bellville, taken a trip to Tangier to retrace his steps in Interzone. Despite having had the go-ahead from Recorded Picture development, it was not until 1989 that Cronenberg was free from other committments and began work on his adaptation.

The result was not a film of the novel, but more of an impressionistic biopic which fused sections of *The Naked Lunch* and *The Exterminator* with sections of William Lee's life as both writer and drug addict. In effect, it is a study of the creative process – the demons that drive it and the twisted erotics of writing. 'The act of writing is not very interesting cinematically,' said Cronenberg. 'It's an interior act.

In order to convey the experience of writing to someone who hasn't written, you have to be outrageous. You have to turn it inside out and make it physical and exterior.' Consequently the film gives us typewriters that metamorphose into assholes, insects acting as the artistic muse, and a world in which writing is both the origin of disease and its antidote.

PETER WELLER plays William Lee.

NAKED LUNCH

In an interview with *Esquire*, Cronenberg compared his relationship to Burroughs with that of Jeff Goldblum's to the insect in his film *The Fly*: 'Here's my conceit. Burroughs and I have been fused in the same telepod together. And what you've got now is the Brundlething, which is my version of *Naked Lunch*. It's a fusion of the two of us, and it really is something that neither one of us would have done alone. Now I don't know which of us is the fly and which is human.'

The metaphor is a telling one, suggesting how Cronenberg's art resurfaces as autobiography as well as implying how the cinematic process often mimics its own subject. Ironically enough, it also echoes Burroughs's own desire to 'schlupp' – to fuse with the other so that the identities of both blur into one. Having failed to schlupp with Ginsberg more than thirty years earlier, he became an unwitting participant of the very same process, this time instigated by a heterosexual Canadian.

And yet for all the talk about teleportation and identity-dissolve, the fact remains that *Naked Lunch* is one of Cronenberg's least forceful films. It is not so much that it is unfaithful to the book, but rather that it almost seems unfaithful to itself. In an otherwise laudatory overview of Cronenberg's career, the critic David Thomson wrote that *Naked Lunch* seemed casual by comparison....The use of Burroughs was dry and inventive, and the film as a whole took drugs for granted in a way movies still find hard. But it had less kick than any other Cronenberg film. He seemed a little tamed, or perhaps to be marking time. The dilemma is a measure of where the medium stands.'

It may also be a measure of where Burroughs stands. For the irony is that many of his other films are far more Burroughsian than the one that is actually about him. The S&M techno-fest that is *Videodrome* brings together the novelist's fascinated repulsion with the potency of the image with a scopophiliac's desire to witness it. Again, *Dead Ringers* acts out the idea of desire as a disease – the mirrors that we find in each other reflecting back at us a desperate (lack of) autonomy. Neither film could have been made without Burroughs – it is as though he is their cinematic ghost-writer. In *Naked Lunch*, however, there is a lack-lustre sense of purpose, as though, having hunted down his Great White Whale, Cronenberg is uncertain what to do with it.

The point seems to be that Burroughs's impact is to influence a sensibility, rather than invite any imitation. 'It was,' said Cronenberg, 'very cathartic for me to write the script of *Naked Lunch*, because I started to write Burroughsian stuff, and almost felt for a moment, "Well, if Burroughs dies, I'll write his next book."' The result suggests the opposite, that Burroughsian influences are at their strongest when they are never actually cited, and that the full glare of his work is perhaps best appreciated by the shadows that it casts.

A writer like Raymond Chandler has spawned a whole generation of acolytes, many of whom have surpassed him to an extent that renders him clichéd and formulaic.

WILLIAM BURROUGHS

THE NAKED LUNCH

William S. Burroughs recording *Naked Lunch*

Septembre, 1994

Hemingway also has had more than his fair share of imitators, and has become a point of comparison against which their work can be judged. Yet both of these writers intended to lay down a blueprint for fiction, a coherent philosophy of composition that would take their work in its given direction. The problem faced by aspiring Burroughs copyists is that they are confronted with texts that write against themselves – a modus *in*operandi, if you like. Burroughs defies imitation because he defies himself, constructing an aesthetic that is born out of its own eradication. Burroughs's writing is the expression of a compromised nihilism, an act of sabotage that collapses every time it is articulated.

This is surely why those attempts to write like Burroughs cannot help but read like parodies of him. A writer like Kathy Acker may well employ cut-up, pastiche and pornography in her work. But the fact that she chooses to embrace strategies which, for him, are acts of disavowal means that her work occupies the peculiar status of aspiring to a condition from which his is trying to escape. Put another way, if Burroughs was about breaking rules, his copyists are concerned with learning them. To do so seems as fake as copying someone else's suicide note.

Chapter 12

It is a seductive paradox that Burroughs is out of imitation's reach whilst simultaneously wielding the most far-reaching of influences. Nowhere is this more evident than in his impact on pop. In transferring his world-view from writing to sound, from narrative to lyric, his work is insinuated into the grain of the music. Writing like Burroughs may be an act of simulation, but for the musician it becomes a form of creative translation. It is the difference between aspiration and appropriation, between following in someone's footsteps and dancing in them.

Of course, Burroughs is not alone in being swept up by pop's plunder. The Beats' relationship with Dylan was one of continuing cross-fertilization, and Kerouac's ghost still haunts the music of bands like the 10,000 Maniacs. Yet no writer has proved as eclectic as Burroughs in his influence on pop, leaving his mark on a whole range of movements from Punk to Techno, Hip-Hop to Grunge.

What are we to make of such breadth, of the fact that so many signatures otherwise in conflict can co-exist upon the same icon? The answer, I would suggest, is to be found in the schizophrenia that characterizes both the impetus of pop and the allure of the writer.

PUNKS
Photo: Erica Echenberg

(AT BONDS)

THE CLASH
Photo: Ebet Roberts

GRUNGE
Photo: Leon Morris

HIP HOP - MISC.

IGGY POP
Photo: Ebet Roberts 8619

DAVID BOWIE

NIRVANA

NEW YORK DOLLS

Keith Richards
ROLLING STONES
Photo: Chuck Boyd

Print File®
ARCHIVAL PRESERVERS
P.O. BOX 607638 • ORLANDO, FL 32860
DATE:
ASSIGNMENT:

From Punk to
Techno, Hip-Hop
to Grunge,
Iggy Pop,
David Bowie,
the Velvet
Underground and
the rest,
Burroughs's
lifestyle puts
the combined
efforts of
Keiths Moon and
Richards to
shame.

On the one hand, rock music is fuelled by an aesthetic of authenticity – the 'walked-it-like-he-talked-it' myth of the messenger at the edge. On the other, pop feeds off the playfulness of its own surface, a delight in the artifice of its own projection. Pop demands that we take Iggy Pop seriously for living within his songs, whilst at the same time paying homage to David Bowie for staying outside his. Hip critics knelt before the Velvet Underground for blurring the boundaries between art and life, yet celebrated Roxy Music for highlighting the distinction.

Pop music's drama is played out between the witness we want to believe in and the cool judgement of the disinterested Inquisitor. It is a space that allows for the mad Puritan and the honest crook, selling itself as The Real Thing *and* a False Prophet all in the time that it takes to change a record.

What Burroughs offers is a figure who embodies pop's repertoire of identities. Here is someone who pursued the hedonistic delights of appetite to their most rock-ish excesses. Burroughs's lifestyle puts the combined efforts of Keiths Moon and Richards to shame. If ever anyone fulfilled Walt Whitman's dictum 'I was the witness/I suffered/I was there', it is surely him. Yet he also manages to offer up the flip-side of authenticated experience – the knowing disingenuousness that constitutes rock's other beloved self. The strung-out oblivion that nurtures pop's more self-destructive fantasies comes dressed in a suit and a haircut that fuels its love of the arbiter. Having displayed his credentials as a Rolling Stone, he switches to the role of the art-school geek. If rock's momentum is Janus-like, Burroughs is able to incorporate both, precisely by being neither.

Burroughs's suitability for pop's hall of infamy predates his actual musical collaborations. His profile featured on the Beatles' *Sgt Pepper* sleeve – an ironic cameo in a psychedelic experiment for which, as we have seen, Burroughs had little sympathy. Heavy Metal first made its entree into popular culture via *The Naked Lunch*, a novel in which Donald Fagen first encountered a dildo referred to as Steely Dan – a term he later borrowed for his band in 1972. The experimental outfit The Soft Machine took their name from Burroughs's third novel. Clearly, music had adopted him long before he put voice to vinyl.

In 1967 Burroughs appeared on the Beatles' *Sgt Pepper* sleeve.

In 1983 Burroughs provided the guest vocals on Laurie Anderson's *Mister Heartbreak* album – a musically accompanied monologue for a track called 'Sharkey's Night'. In 1981 he had gone on tour with the New York performance artist as well as the poet John Giorno. Rumour has it that the first time they met Burroughs thought Anderson was a boy – a testament to her androgynous mystique rather than to his own myopia.

In retrospect it seems fitting that it was Anderson who made music's first real use of Burroughs, as her work evokes similar spectres. Passionately disembodied, Anderson's songs patrol the area where the antiseptic commandeers the erotic. She foregrounds the materiality of her music, all synthezised harmonies and stuttering rhythms, reminding us that sound is clinical as well as visceral. It is the sound that rap would make if it were driven by curiosity rather than fury; one that the critic Greil Marcus described as 'an implacable, hysterical hesitation: hesitation as a form of anticipation'.

Over a staccato, almost militaristic, bass line Burroughs speaks of a night full of promise for his protagonist – a hotel receptionist who has abandoned his post and gone to join the revellers. It is a song whose mystery lies in its ellipses – the less we are told, the more we are invited to ponder. If Burroughs's art was to rub out the word, Anderson's is the Word Kept-Back – the carving out of silences that meaning rushes to fill.

Three years later Burroughs was to make an appearance in Anderson's concept video *Home of the Brave*. The role was that of her dancing partner, although he laconically dismissed it by later saying, 'I still don't know how to tango.' More significantly, the tango in question was danced to a song entitled 'Language Is a Virus'.

The producer of *Mister Heartbreak* was Bill Laswell, and in 1989 his band, Material, recorded an album entitled *Seven Souls*. The concept was based around *The Western Lands* and interspersed readings from Burroughs with a form of jazz fusion that had a distinctively Middle Eastern feel. The slippage between music and text can be seen as an extension of the cut-up – another way of making language a stranger to itself by welding it to an alien medium. What is mesmerizing about the album is the way in which each track refutes the categories of either text or song. They are neither simply words put to music nor lyrics with an implicit form. In the terminology of Roland Barthes each song hovers between 'geno' and 'pheno', conflating both forms to a condition that he described as 'the body in the voice as it sings, the hand as it writes, the limb as it performs'. This sense of the holistic is reminiscent of Burroughs's nostalgia for the hieroglyph – a form in which artistic expression side-steps the descriptive, and instead becomes an act that is its own articulation. Like the Egyptian hieroglyphs, music does not ask us to choose between form and content. The two become co-dependent to the point of a Siamese connection.

In a bizarre sense, then, *Seven Souls* is closer to the spirit of *The Western Lands* than the novel itself. If Burroughs's novel imprisoned as it created, Material are able to cut free from the limits of language by providing it with their own punctuation. If music has its unique diction then 'the writer', in Burroughs's words, 'makes a soundless bow and disappears into the alphabet'. Burroughs's skill lies in his ability to reappear even as he vanishes.

Hamburg, 1990. The opening of *The Black Rider.*

Hal Willner first met Burroughs when he was the music co-ordinator for *Saturday Night Live* – a 1981 appearance in which the writer read from *The Soft Machine* and *The Naked Lunch* as Willner played a recording of 'The Star Spangled Banner'. Seven years later, as he recalls, he 'arrived in Lawrence, Kansas, with a portable DAT machine to record WSB. We came with no script. For three days and nights we improvised...recording William reading from his lecture archives; loose conversations; various poetry; selections from some of his better-known works. The result, *Dead City Radio*, was released in 1990.

Though it was essentially a spoken word album, various recitals feature accompaniment from John Cale, Donald Fagen, Chris Stein and Sonic Youth, among others. Yet the momentum for the record, the structure that holds it together, is Burroughs's voice. As flat as the prairies, at times gnarled and glutinous, it is a voice rich in a

196

history that it has both absorbed and discarded. He talks of the 'Apocalypse' in a tone that relishes its own indifference to its portents. 'The Lord's Prayer' is delivered without any of the sneering satire one might expect, but with a solemnity that reshapes it as being sacrilegious in itself. 'When you listen to the voice, let the voice listen to you,' writes Willner in his sleeve notes, and certainly the effect is one of someone eavesdropping on a dialogue we didn't know we were having.

Nirvana were the quintessence of wounded abjection, their songs an expression of disgusted rage at their own impotence. Kurt Cobain had been a fan of Burroughs ever since high school.

As the title suggests, the album is a transfusion of technology's life-blood into the veins of mortality – a bit like broadcasting a talk show from a cemetery. Having written of 'The Place of Dead Roads', Burroughs here conjures up the conversations that take place there.

It was Grauerholz who suggested bringing Burroughs together with The Disposable Heroes of Hiphoprisy for their 1993 record, *Spare Ass Annie*. Routines such as 'The Talking Asshole' and 'Dr Benway Operates' are propelled along by a mixture of guitar funk and orchestral samples. As George Eckart pointed out in his review for *Diversions*, 'Even though the tales don't necessarily connect, the Heroes make the whole album stick together as one, creating a funky, surreal and absorbing trip through Burroughs' twisted literary vision.' In his 'Words of Advice For Young People', Burroughs ironizes his own status as elderly statesman, rasping that they 'should never trust a religious sonofabitch' in a way that cloaks the serious in the sententious.

The aesthetic logic that leads hip-hop to Burroughs is a shared appreciation of theft. In its samples, remixes and disregard for copyright, hip-hop celebrates music's ability to plunder the past in order to reconstruct the present. As Burroughs wrote in 'Les Voleurs',

Everything belongs to the inspired and dedicated thief....They supplicate him from the bored minds of school children, from the prisons of uncritical veneration, from dead museums and dusty archives....He must assure himself of the quality of the merchandise and its suitability for his purpose before he conveys the supreme honor and benediction of his theft. . . .We are not responsible. Steal anything in sight.

This passage could well stand as hip-hop's manifesto, and certainly the very name, The Disposable Heroes, suggests that they do not consider themselves exempt. Their bid is not for longevity, but for a pursuit of the moment – a moment that may be constructed from the stolen sounds that have gone before. As with The Wild Boys, there is a sense within hip-hop that history belongs to those who can use it.

If the practitioners of hip-hop cast themselves as rock music's vandals, the grunge bands flaunted their status as its casualties. Kurt Cobain's Nirvana were the quintessence of such wounded abjection, their songs an expression of disgusted rage at their own impotence. The critics Simon Reynolds and Joy Press have written of 'Cobain's divided impulses. On the one hand, the desire to make a break with the suffocating comfort of domesticity. On the other, an urge to refuse manhood in a world where most manifestations of masculinity are loathsome, a desire to be infantilized and emasculated.' Burroughs was the natural father of these dysfunctional infants – a figure who proved that it was possible to grow old without having to 'grow up'.

Cobain had been a fan of Burroughs ever since high school and, through their mutual friend Thor Lindsay (a producer at Tim Kerr records), provided a mangled guitar backdrop to a recital called 'The "Priest", They Called Him'. The track, approximately ten minutes long, tells of a junkie priest who on Christmas Eve comes across a suitcase in the street that contains a dismembered body. The result was not particularly memorable – Cobain's guitar takes Burroughs at his word, rather than playing against it – although their meeting was more than amicable. Burroughs recalled that, 'There was something boyish about him, fragile and engagingly lost'; later he remarked to Grauerholz, 'There's something wrong with that boy. He frowns for no good reason.'

In April 1994 Cobain put a shotgun in his mouth and blew his brains out.

In his collaboration with Tom Waits and Robert Wilson, Burroughs turned to the nineteenth-century myths of Germanic folklore. *The Black Rider* began life as an opera – it premiered at the Thalia Theatre in Hamburg in 1990 and continues to be performed in repertory today – Tom Waits re-recorded his compositions for the album released in 1993. Burroughs wrote the libretto in its entirety, contributed lyrics to many of Waits's songs and, as Waits wrote in his sleeve notes, '[provided] the branch this bundle would swing from. His cut-up text and open process of finding a language for this story became a river of words for me to draw from'. The concept was an ideal vehicle for both concerned. Pitched somewhere between Bedlam and the carnival, it allowed Waits to pursue his interest in vaudevillian nightmare – a

In 1994 Cobain blew his brains out.

200

process that he had begun in 'Swordfishtrombones' and carried on into the staging of his album *Frank's Wild Years*. For Burroughs, the story resonated with the kind of Faustian motifs he had grown familiar with via his own Ugly Spirit.

The Black Rider was first incarnated in *Das Gespensterbuch*, a body of Romantic literature first published around 1810, and found its most famous expression in Carl Maria von Weber's opera *Der Freishütz*. The tale concerns a young clerk's bid to marry a forester's daughter; in order to win her hand he must first triumph in a shooting contest. A hopeless marksman, he is approached by a 'dark horseman' who is in possession of magic bullets that are guaranteed to hit whatever they are fired at. The Devil, however, is to have control over the final bullet. The suitor succeeds in winning the contest, but on the wedding day the Devil calls in his marker. The newly-wed shoots at a wooden dove, but the result is that he kills his bride.

In his collaboration with Tom Waits and Robert Wilson, Burroughs turned to the nineteenth-century myths of Germanic folklore.

The parallels between this fable and Burroughs's shooting of Joan are glaringly powerful, without being limited to them.

As with his shotgun art, Burroughs's empathy for the Black Rider invites personal speculation whilst artistically refuting it. Burroughs moves between biography and fiction in such a way as to suggest that the two are synonymous. The task that he sets us is not to separate life from art, but to wonder at the nature of the contract between them. As Waits said, 'Burroughs found some of the branches of the story, and let them grow into more metaphorical things in all of our lives every day that, in fact, are deals with the devil that we've made. What is cunning about those deals is that we're not aware we've made them. And when they come to fruition, we are shocked and amazed.'

The Black Rider had its American debut at the Brooklyn Academy of Music in New York, and was also performed in Vienna, Paris, Amsterdam and Berlin. As an album it constitutes Burroughs's most enduring musical contribution to date. It is a haunting *danse macabre*, an evocation of the dark melancholy of the Faust myth as well as its demonic edges. Waits and Burroughs complement each other with a dramatic unease, like two inmates forced to share a cell. John Rockwell in the *New York Times* heralded it as a cross between *The Threepenny Opera* and *The Rocky Horror Picture Show*, whilst Jackie Wullschlager wrote that it transforms 'children's drawings into three-dimensional monstrosities....Waits' sarcastic ballads, full of folk and blues and rock, call back the scarred idealism and mock simplicity of Kurt Weill, while Burroughs' monosyllabic banality has here found the setting which makes it seem perfect.'

It is also a cabaret that is forced to take itself seriously – the sound of laughter in the dark attempting to stifle its own hysteria.

In the figure of Burroughs, rock music finds someone equal to its bleakest visions and maverick ploys. His disinterest allows him to carry off their strategies whilst never being carried away by them. He does not confer approval on his collaborators, so much as anomaly – a space in which incongruities are allowed to seek out their own harmony. It is as though the less he strives to be an innovator in pop, the more he allows musicians to innovate round him. The appeal of his recordings is that most of them sound as if they have been made against his better judgement – or in the absence of any judgement at all. This is not to say that he is without discernment, but rather that there is an incidental quality to his presence on record, as though he has stumbled into a studio, unaware of the esteem in which those present hold h[...]

Burroughs will not be remembered as a rock star any more than David Bowie will go down in history as an actor. And yet he continues to be heralded as a rock sensibility – a figure whose fluidity and strategies of dissent permeate certain musical mentalities to which he has particular allegiance.

Burroughs may be the only American author whose name has been used to denote a sound. 'Burroughsian' does not merely refer to the content of a record, but to its actual condition – the attitude on which it is predicated.

13

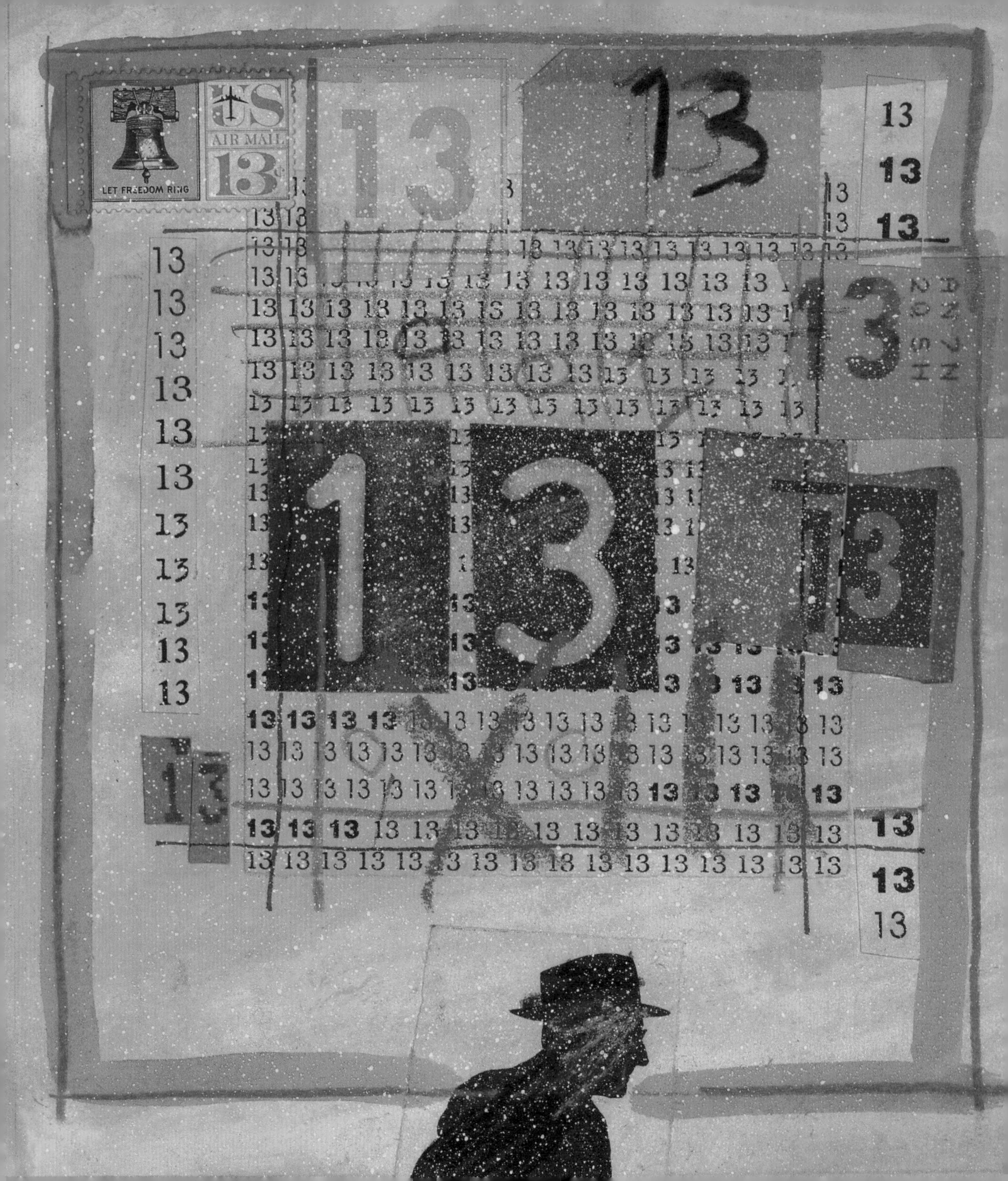
LET FREEDOM RING
US
AIR MAIL
13¢
13

Chapter 13

Amidst the blizzard of images and influences that circulated around the man in his last years, it was easy to forget that there existed a lower-case Burroughs at the centre of it all – a fragile old man in his eighties who lived his life irrespective of the legend it had generated.

Speculation was naturally rife. If rumours were to be believed, in his last few years Burroughs had become the Unabomber, fled to Central America, returned to being a junkie and was a demented loon who would shoot any visitors who strayed near his porch. The reality was more mundane. Barry Miles spent Thanksgiving with him in 1996 and told of a lifestyle that moved placidly between routine and relaxation. At 9 a.m. one of the employees from Burroughs Communications came to fix his breakfast, just as another would arrive in the early evening to cook his supper. The days were spent either painting or writing, interspersed with target-practice at a nearby friend's shooting range. At 4 p.m. the first vodka and Coke of the day was eagerly consumed, although the booze would be moderated until he went to bed around nine.

William Burroughs as himself

© Jon Blumb, 1994.
835½ Massachusetts St.

206

There were a ridiculous number of interview requests, most of which were refused, although he could do little about the number of diehard fans who would make unannounced visits. One of them camped out in his yard; others were lucky enough to receive a brief audience. None of them came away with anything they didn't know before. It was not as though Burroughs had nothing new to say, but there was a problem in finding anything new to ask him.

William S. Burroughs as himself, 1994.

His interest in sex had waned, and his passion was reserved for his cats, of which in these years he had six. As he told Victor Bockris, '[Cats] reflect you in a very deep way. They just opened up a whole area of compassion in me. I remember lying in my bed weeping and weeping to think that a nuclear catastrophe would destroy them.'

Even in his attitude to his pets, Burroughs brought together the paranoia of the atomic age with an almost mystical attachment for ancient Egypt's most potent symbol.

For a man who seemed to have set out to defy the laws of medicine, the elderly Burroughs apparently remained in remarkably good health. In the summer of 1991 he underwent a triple heart bypass, but within a month was walking around unaided. In the following year he made a suitably bizarre attempt to heal his psyche. He told Bockris that he could still sense the presence of the Ugly Spirit, that 'When I go into my psyche, at a certain point I meet a very hostile, very strong force. It's as definite as someone attacking me in a bar. We usually come to a standoff.'

In March 1992 he decided to fight back. With the help of Ginsberg,

Burroughs underwent a ceremony of cleansing – a ritual that had originated with the Sioux Indians and was performed for him by a Navajo shaman called Melvin Betsellie. Without a trace of irony, Ginsberg and Burroughs stripped naked and sat around a coal fire whilst the shaman chanted, prayed and exorcized the evil that he could sense within him. Burroughs certainly felt that the process had been a success, later telling Ginsberg:

That was much better than anything psychoanalysts have come up with…something definite there was being touched upon…getting to the moment when whatever it was gained access. And also to the name of the spirit. Just to know that it's the Ugly Spirit. That's a great step. Because the spirit doesn't want its name to be known.

What is of interest in this episode is not whether or not the shamanistic rituals of the Sioux have any therapeutic value, but that Burroughs should have wanted to believe that they possess some. For a writer whose touchstone has been one of radical scepticism, there still existed within him a desire or a leap of blind faith. It was as though Burroughs's deep-seated mistrust was less about standing back from belief systems, and more about discovering which ones it was worth stepping into. As with his use of Scientology, there was a naïveté about Burroughs's interests – a willingness to confront philosophies at face value without ever taking them at their word.

Two years after his Native American Awakening, Burroughs

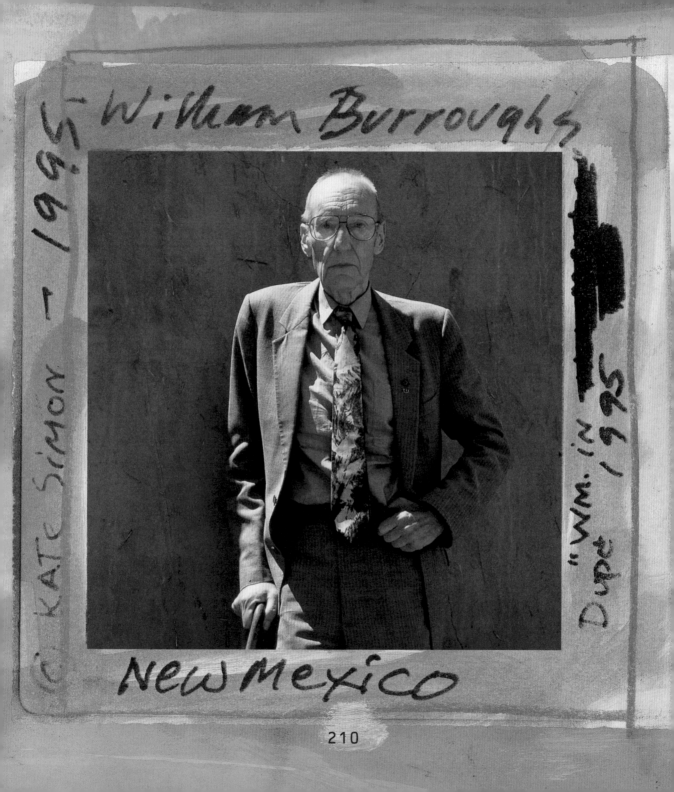

© KATE SIMON — 1995
William Burroughs
"WM. in Dupe 1995"
New Mexico

210

appeared in a television commercial for Nike training shoes. The juxtaposition of spiritual cleansing with naked commerce suggests a contradiction that no other icon could balance. The cry of 'sell out' greets any artist who is seen to prostitute his or her talent merely to shift product. The difference with Burroughs was that no one can be sure what he was selling – irony, indifference or integrity. Indeed, watching the Nike commercial one gets the impression that it is they who had to buy into Burroughs, and not the other way round. Far from being the appropriation of a marginalized icon, it was an acknowledgement that his image was always beyond their grasp. It was as though there was nothing that Burroughs could do that would be 'Un-Burroughsian', no act or statement that would have tainted his credibility. He existed not at the limits of culture, but in its wilderness – a nomad who could never be accused of having deserted his home.

As Burroughs wrote in his *Book of Dreams*,

Ted Morgan's biography starts with a basic misconception: 'Literary Outlaw'. To be an outlaw you must first have a base in law to reject and get out of. I never had such a base. I never had a place I could call home that meant any more than a key to a house, apartment, or hotel room....

Am I an alien? Alien from what exactly? Perhaps my home is the dream city, more real than my so-called waking life precisely because it has no relation to waking life.

"All the News That's Fit to Print"

The New York Times

Late Edition
New York: Today, cloudy, a few showers High 66. Tonight, mild, showers. Low 54. Tomorrow, a morning shower, windy. High 71. Yesterday, high 56, low 47. Details on page 44

VOL. CXLVI .. No. 50,754   Copyright © 1997 The New York Times   NEW YORK, SUNDAY, APRIL 6, 1997 $3 beyond the greater New York metropolitan area $2.50

Allen Ginsberg, Master Poet Of Beat Generation, Dies at 70

By WILBORN HAMPTON

Allen Ginsberg, the poet laureate of the Beat Generation whose "Howl!" became a manifesto for the sexual revolution and a cause célèbre for free speech in the 1950's, eventually earning its author a place in America's literary pantheon, died early yesterday. He was 70 and lived in the East Village, in Manhattan.

He died of liver cancer at his apartment, Bill Morgan, a friend and the poet's archivist, said.

Mr. Morgan said that Mr. Ginsberg wrote right to the end. "He's working on a lot of poems, talking to old friends," Mr. Morgan said on Friday. "He's in very good spirits. He wants to write poetry and finish his life's work."

William S. Burroughs, one of Mr. Ginsberg's lifelong friends and a fellow Beat, said that Mr. Ginsberg's death was "a great loss to me and everybody."

"We were friends for more than years," Mr. Burroughs said. " was a great person with worl influence. He was a pioneer o ness and a lifelong model of He stood for freedom of exp and for coming out of all the long before others did. He h ence because he said wha lieved. I will miss him."

As much through the str his own irrepressible person through his poetry, Mr. G provided a bridge between t derground and the Transcen He was as comfortable in the rams of Indian gurus in the 1960 he had been in the Beat coffeehous of the preceding decade.

A ubiquitous presence at the love-

Continued on Page 42, Column 1

ns and be-ins that marked the drug-orient d counterculture of the Flower Childr years, Mr. Ginsberg was also in guard of the political prote hey helped spawn. He marcl war in Vietnam, the C.I.A. a Iran, among other causes.

If his early verse shocked America with its celebration ity and drugs, his involvem kept him in the public eye at tion to his critics. But thro Ginsberg maintained a sort

He was known around the world as a master of the outrageous. He read his poetry and played finger cymbals at the Albert Hall in London; he was expelled from Cuba after saying he found Che Guevara "cute"; he sang duets with Bob Dylan, and he chanted "Hare Krishna" on William F. Buckley Jr.'s television program. As the critic John Leonard observed in a 1988 appreciation: "He is of course a social bandit. But he is a nonviolent social bandit."

Or as the narrator in Saul Bellow's "Him With His Foot in His Mouth" said of Mr. Ginsberg: "Under all this self-revealing candor is purity of heart. And the only authentic living representative of American Transcendentalism is that fat-breasted, bald, bearded homosexual in smeared goggles, innocent in his uncleanness."

J. D. McClatchy

The Yale Re berg was a his gen literar

the name Eugene Brooks. Eugene, a lawyer, survives.

Recalling his parents in a 1985 interview, Mr. Ginsberg said:

"They were old-fashioned delicatessen philosophers. My father would the house either recitin and Longfellow under h ing T. S. Eliot for ruinh 'obscurantism.' My mot time stories that all we 'The good king rode for saw the suffering worker I grew suspicious of both

An Authorizatio For a Lobotomy

Allen Ginsberg's moth from paranoia and was in hospitals; Mr. Ginsberg si zation for a lobotomy. died in 1956 in Pilgrim St Long Island, he received a that said: "The key is in the is in the sunlight in the wind e, your mother." — get married Allen d ears after her deat sh for Naomi y that man

of you ile I w Gree lea igh ad s

e Beats were creating literary history around Columbia and the West End Café, there was a dangerous undercurrent to their activities. Mr. Carr spent a brie time in jail for manslaught Mr. for a

There ed a Mr. s ll h

There Beatniks were writ John Clel beat is to ty lookin out of di ment with

Mr. Gi the Beats "Whitm the mater ened by would win We're go see. Only sponsibili feel. That trying to c

On an literary r have to b candid." candid.

As he poem, wh

McCarth

Amer Amer cer

Amer Amer loo Amer

Mr. Gi the prin William and Wil new met he said, your he three or sentence lines eac

His di only gav Dickey i with Alle seem as

Trav For I

Mr. Gi with "H next two India to and to v dissiden

to give up the what would make me happy? g hung his gray flannel suit in the closer d went to San Francisco wit unemploy- Francisco e literary e corner nghetti's blishing

g also literary h — an Snyder, Robert so met mpan-

berg's most famous poem, was dedicated Solomon, and begins:

I saw the best minds of my generation destroyed by madness, starving hysterical naked, dragging themselves through the negro streets at dawn looking for an angr fix, angelheaded hipsters burning for the ancient heavenly connection to the starry dynamo in the machinery of night

his first major work from San Francisco was "Howl!" The long-running poem expressed the anxieties and ideals of a generation alienated from mainstream society. "Howl!," which was to become Mr. Gins-

Mr. Ginsberg read the poem to a gathering arranged by Mr. Rexroth, and those present never forgot the poem, its author the occasion.

Mr. Rexroth's wife privately distributed mimeographed 50-copy edition of "How" and in 1956, Mr. Ferlinghetti published "Howl! and Other Poems" in what he called his "pocket poets series."

With its open and often vivid celebration of homosexuality and eroticism, "How" was impounded by United States Cust

On 5 April 1997, Allen Ginsberg died of liver cancer in New York at the age of seventy. Only two days earlier he had gone public with his illness, and was expected to live for another twelve months. Ginsberg's death may have been premature, but he prepared for it as some kind of art form. According to Bill Morgan – his bibliographer and unofficial spokesman – Ginsberg returned from the hospital after his diagnosis and worked on a series of poems late into the night. Just as Leary died on the Net – a cyber-death for someone for whom reality had always been virtual – so Ginsberg died to the sound of his own scansion. 'Death & Fame' was a celebration of his own imagined funeral – an event that would remind his lovers, friends and followers that, 'Everyone knew they were part of "History" except the deceased/who never knew exactly what was happening even when I was alive.'

Burroughs and Ginsberg had known each other for nearly half a century, and the younger poet had probably been the only constant in the other's erratic wanderings. As the tributes and obituaries flooded in, Burroughs paid his own respects by recording a short statement which was played at a Ginsberg tribute in Los Angeles in 1997.

It is fair to say that, in the process of discovering America, its writers have always been in the business of (re)inventing it. Whether it has been Jefferson's agrarian Eden, Fitzgerald's bruised innocence or Bellow's moronic inferno, American literature has transformed its landscapes into a cultural experiment. It is a stage on which its artists are able to dramatize possibilities, one in which ideas enact their own complexities. The sanctity of the individual, the democratic vista, American Dreams and Awakenings – all have been brought to life, their creators often aghast at the lives they then lead.

On 5 April 1997, Allen Ginsberg died of liver cancer in New York at the age of seventy. Burroughs and Ginsberg had known each other for nearly half a century.

BUR-ROSE

214

Like Ahab's pursuit of the Whale, or the glare of Gatsby's green light, America is the place where the vast thrill of potential rubs shoulders with the threat of its outcome.

In the figure of William Burroughs, America finds one of the most perverse versions of itself to be proposed this century. He assimilated every fabric of his culture and re-presented it in its deformity. He was as American as the electric chair – an artist who attempted to execute his culture by embracing everything it held dear. He claimed individualism but not its conscience, liberty but not duty, extremity without censure. Burroughs took American ideology and robbed it of its piety, exposing the contract that is its Constitution as one that is open to the most bizarre of negotiations.

Like America herself, Burroughs may only have had

Burroughs at home in Lawrence, Kansas — as American as the electric chair.

Epilogue

On Sunday, 3 August 1997, Burroughs's Internet Homepage received the following announcement: 'News Flash: William Burroughs has finally figured out how to leave the flesh behind and assimilate with it all.'

It had been a heart attack, one that his New York agent, Ira Silverberg, described as 'sudden. William was in fine health.'

Sudden or not, Burroughs's death was one that in many ways had been well rehearsed in his work. Whether it be Dutch Schultz's *Last Words* or those of Billy the Kid, Burroughs had long displayed a fascination – even a yearning – for a sense of an ending. Death, for Burroughs, signalled release – a state that could liberate his characters from the limits of their humanity. His enduring interest in necromancy gives his own death an ironic charm. If Burroughs defied the Moral Majority by simply living so long, he then rubbed their noses in it by dying so peacefully.

The obituaries were filed on the Monday, most of them focusing on the notoriety of *Naked Lunch*, the shooting of Joan and his friendship with the Beats. J. G. Ballard wrote of how 'his weird genius was the perfect mirror of these times, and made him the most important and original writer since the Second World War', adding that, 'Now we are left with the career novelists.'

What united the tributes was a general feeling that Burroughs's death was also the death of an era – the passing on of the last vestiges of gunslinging America. And yet as its culture seems more and more driven to re-define its own boundaries, there is another sense in which Burroughs's project has never appeared so urgent. His voice echoes throughout American literature's white noise, its meltdown of genres and infinite jests. His repertoire of selves can be found scattered amongst pop music's disjointed body, just as his cut-up can be heard in the sound of the sampler. Far from being the end of an era, Burroughs has been instrumental in creating the one in which we now live.

The man may be dead, his legacy has never been more alive.

Burroughs at the Bunker,
21 September 1995.

William S. Burroughs, the Beat Writer Who Distilled His Raw Nightmare Life, Di

By RICHARD SEVERO

lliam S. Burroughs, a renegade writer
Beat Generation who stunned readers
inspired adoring cultists with his 1959
"Naked Lunch," died on Saturday
ng at Lawrence Memorial Hospital in
nce, Kan. He was 83.

cause of his death was a heart attack
he suffered on Friday, his publicist, Ira
berg, said.

er the years, Mr. Burroughs had lived
uch places as New York, London, Paris,
co City and Tangier. But since 1981 he
tained a house in Lawrence, where he
simply with three cats and indulged
interests in painting and photography
collecting and discharging firearms.

Burroughs had undergone triple by-
urgery in 1991. He quit smoking after
eration. And though he continued to
from a leaky heart valve, from all
ts he regained robust health quickly
man of his years.

recovery was all the more noteworthy
he had spent so many of his younger
engulfed in narcotics addiction, an
ative so demanding that in 1954, while
in London, he sold his typewriter to
heroin, although he kept working in
nd. He spent years experimenting
rugs as well as with sex, which he
d in with men, women and children.
ked Lunch," first published in Paris,
er by Grove Press in New York, was
as a masterly definition of what was
hough the critics were not sure how
ne the definition. Herbert Gold, writ-
n The New York Times, said that he
was "less a novel than a series of
, puns, epigrams — all hovering about
licit subject matter of making out on
while not making out in either work or
Mr. Gold called the book "booty
back from a nightmare."
week said that "Naked Lunch" pos-
a "strange genius" and was a mas-
e "but a totally insane and anarchic
d it can only be diminished by at-
to give it a social purpose or value
er."

A Man Who 'Simply Doesn't Like' People

His work was not for traditionalists who
loved a well-developed narrative. Dame
Edith Sitwell was among those who de-
murred from the critics' praise, denouncing
"Naked Lunch" as psychopathological filth.
And even those who admired Mr. Burroughs's iconoclasm and his ruthless honesty had to admit that they could see flaws
in the man. He was, in the final analysis, an
alien among aliens, the ultimate odd duck.

"Just because he sleeps with boys, takes
drugs and smokes dope doesn't mean that
he tolerates or supports the majority of
junkies, homosexuals or potheads," wrote
Barry Miles in his 1993 biography, "William
Burroughs," which was subtitled "El Hombre Invisible" and published by Hyperion.
"Bill simply doesn't like most people."

William Seward Burroughs was born on
Feb. 5, 1914, in St. Louis, the son of Mortimer
P. Burroughs, the owner of a plate-glass
company, and Laura Lee Burroughs, who
came from a prominent Southern family.
His grandfather, for whom he was named,
invented the perforated, oil-filled cylinder
that made the Burroughs adding machine
add and invariably get the right answer. The
machine became a standard fixture in small
and large businesses everywhere.

Mr. Burroughs's parents sold their stock
in the Burroughs Company shortly before

igmas of a Gaunt Man

illiam S. Burroughs, in a 1984
le for The New York Times Book
iew, gave his own assessment of
eculiar body of work. Much of it,
rote, "is intended to be funny."
se are among his most important
s:

ie (Ace, 1953)
d Lunch (Olympia, 1959)
Soft Machine (Olympia, 1961)
Ticket that Exploded (Olympia,
2)
Fingers Talk (Calder, 1963)
Yage Letters (with Allen Gins-
g, City Lights, 1963)
Express (Grove Press, 1964)
rminator? (Viking, 1973)
Last Words of Dutch Schultz
king, 1975, from a 1970 film
ipt)
of the Red Night (Holt, Rine-
t & Winston)
Place of Dead Souls (Holt, Rine-
t & Winston)
(Viking, 1985)
Western Lands (Viking, 1987)
one (Viking, 1989)

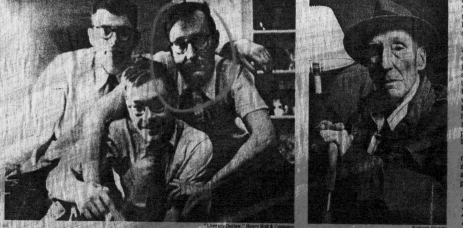

"Literary Outlaw," Henry Holt & Company   Richard Devinki

William S. Burroughs, above at right, in 1953 with his friends and members of the Beat Generation, Lucien Carr, center, and Allen Ginsberg; it was Ginsberg who came up with the title "Naked Lunch" several years later. The author at home in Kansas last year.

For his part, Mr. Burroughs said he
agreed with the writer Mary McCarthy, who
thought that "Naked Lunch," and his other
books, had a deep moral purpose.

"I do definitely mean what I say to be
taken literally, yes, to make people aware of
the true criminality of our times, to wise up
to the marks," Mr. Burroughs told an inter-
viewer in 1970.

Nobody found it especially easy to impose
literality on Mr. Burroughs's sentences, either written or spoken. He described "Naked Lunch" as "a frozen moment when
everyone sees what is on the end of every
fork."

When Mr. Burroughs was a teen-ager, he
read "You Can't Win," an autobiography of
Jack Black, a drifter who took drugs and
pilfered his way through a sordid, predatory
life. The book made a considerable impression on him and became grist for his own
books years later. It was around this time
that he, too, started experimenting with
drugs.

Mr. Burroughs was educated, not happily,
in private schools in St. Louis and in Los
Alamos, N.M. He was sent to Harvard University, which he did not like any better than
he had his preparatory schools, although the
time spent reading pleased him. His favor-
ite writers gave no hint of what was ultimately to come out of his typewriter. They
included Shakespeare, Coleridge and De-
Quincy. Other writers he came to admire
included James Joyce, Joseph Conrad, Jean
Genet, Franz Kafka, Graham Greene and
Raymond Chandler. He received a bacca-
laureate degree from Harvard in 1936.

He took a vacation to Europe after graduation and in Dubrovnik met Ilse Klapper, a
German Jew who had fled the Nazis. She
was stranded, unable to renew her Yugoslav
passport and unable to go to the United
States. To accommodate her, he married
her. They never lived together, and dis-
solved the marriage almost immediately
upon returning to the United States, but they
remained friends. After his return he
worked at many jobs, including bartender,
private detective, factory worker and insect
exterminator. Except for exterminating,
which he rather enjoyed, these jobs bored
him. He later recalled his experiences in
"Exterminator!" published by Viking in
1973.

In the years before World War II, he
returned to Harvard and did some graduate
work in cultural anthropology and ethnolo-
gy. After the war began, he was drafted into
the Army but got out after only three
months. The Miles biography said that Mr.

the stock market crash of 1929, and the
$200,000 they received saw them nicely
through the Depression. It did not leave the
author with much of a legacy; his mother
died in 1970, and what was left of her share
of the estate was $10,000.

When Mr. Burroughs was a teen-ager, he
read "You Can't Win," an autobiography of
Jack Black, a drifter who took drugs and
pilfered his way through a sordid, predatory
life. The book made a considerable impression on him and became grist for his own
books years later. It was around this time
that he, too, started experimenting with
drugs.

Burroughs's mother used her influence to
win his discharge for physical reasons.

Scrawl of 'Naked Lust' Becomes 'Naked Lunch'

By 1944, he had an apartment on Bedford
Street in Greenwich Village and developed
an addiction to heroin. Among those he
befriended in New York in the 1940's were
Allen Ginsberg and Jack Kerouac. It was to
these three and their friends and acquaintances that the term Beat Generation would
later be applied. And it was Ginsberg who,
several years later, inadvertently came up
with the title "Naked Lunch." He got it from
misreading a bit of manuscript in Mr. Burroughs's scrawl, which actually referred to
"naked lust."

Mr. Burroughs's first book, published by
Ace in 1953 under the pseudonym William
Lee, was called "Junkie" and told of his
years as an addict. The writing of "Junkie"
came after what was arguably the saddest
part of Mr. Burroughs's life. He had married Joan Vollmer in 1945, and in 1951 they
were living in Mexico City. He was using
drugs heavily and had returned to Mexico
City from a trip to Ecuador, where he had
tried to learn more about a hallucinogen
called yage. His wife was addicted to Benzedrine and, Barry Miles wrote, did not mind
Mr. Burroughs's homosexual interests. Indeed, she had borne him a son.

Their life in Mexico City was not especially happy. One September afternoon in 1951,
they began to drink with friends. Eventually, Mr. Burroughs, who was quite drunk,
took a handgun out of his travel bag and told
his wife, "It's time for our William Tell act."
There never had been a William Tell act, but
his wife laughed and put a water glass on
her head. Mr. Burroughs fired the gun. The
bullet entered her brain through her fore-
head, killing her instantly. The Mexican
authorities concluded that it was an accident. Mr. Burroughs was convicted only of a
minor charge and served little time in jail.

Years later, he would say that he would
never have become a writer had it not been

for her death. His w
"brought me into cont
the Ugly Spirit and m
lifelong struggle, in w
choice but to write my
The incident did not s
in his introduction to
describes his addictio
junk, eaten it, sniffed
skin-muscle, inserted
tories. The needle is
Burroughs wrote that
was an addict, he did
He said, "I could look a
for eight hours." When
15 years of addiction
phine, a chemical con
Britain.

His son, William, di
roughs is survived by
manager, James Graue
at Lawrence Hospital
phone calls.

Trying to Brea To Simulate L

No other Burroughs
attention of "Naked Lu
always interested the
started inserting share
paragraphs from news
thors into his own prose
wanted to break the p
mally finds in a book
peripheral impressions
itself.

"I don't plan a book c
it's going to end," he to
He readily admitted th
erable overlap of mater

In 1989, he collaborat
"The Black Rider,"
formed at the Brooklyn
by the Thalia Theater o
based on "Der Freischü
Carl Maria von Web
wrote the libretto; To
songs, and it was stage
It was also produced in
In his later years, he
great deal of time as a
pher.

Only a week before hi
helping to prepare sele
published next year by
Silverberg, the publicis
of a novel, "The Third N
uled by Grove Press for
year Viking Press reissu
A Book of Dreams."

In a rare interview
Burroughs told The New
made entries in a journ
given up formal writing
guess I have run out of
also said that he had te
painting. "I don't want
myself," he said.

Several of his friends
and contemporaries ha
two years, including T
bert Huncke and Allen G
of his life, Mr. Burroug
mistic about the future
"Ghost of a Chance," h
struction of the rain for
tures and wrote: "All p
for more and more dev
with less and less of t
priceless ingredient —
A vast mudslide of soul

at 83

Far left:
New York Times
obituary, 4
August 1997.
Left: Burroughs
approaches the
end. *The Village
Voice* reported
in their
Burroughs
obituary of 12
August 1997
'Live fast,
die old'.

Bibliography

Burroughs texts (solo)
Junkie, New York: Ace Books, 1953
The Naked Lunch, Paris: Olympia Press, 1961
(the 'The' was dropped from the US edition, New York: Grove Press, 1962)
The Soft Machine, Paris: Olympia Press, 1961
(US edition, New York: Grove Press, 1966)
The Ticket that Exploded, Paris: Olympia Press, 1962
(US edition, New York: Grove Press, 1967)
Nova Express, New York: Grove Press, 1964
The Wild Boys, New York: Grove Press, 1971
Exterminator!, New York: Viking Press, 1973
The Last Words of Dutch Schultz, New York: Viking Press, 1975
Port of Saints, Berkeley: Blue Wind Press, 1980
Cities of the Red Night, New York: Holt, 1981
The Place of Dead Roads, New York: Holt, 1984
The Burroughs File, San Francisco: City Lights Press, 1984
The Adding Machine, London: John Calder, 1985
Queer, New York: Viking Penguin, 1985
The Western Lands, New York: Viking Penguin, 1987
Interzone, ed. James Grauerholz, New York: Viking Press, 1989
Blade Runner, a Movie, Berkeley: Blue Wind Press, 1990
Ghost of Chance, New York: High Risk/Serpent's Tail, 1995
My Education: A Book of Dreams, New York: Viking Penguin, 1995

Interviews/Letters

The Job: Interviews with William Burroughs, Daniel Odier,
New York: Grove Press, 1974
With William Burroughs: A Report from the Bunker,
Victor Bockris, New York: Seaver Books, 1981
The Letters of William S. Burroughs, ed. Oliver Harris,
New York: Viking Press, 1993

Collaborations

Minute to Go (with Sinclair Beiles, Gregory Corso and Brion Gysin),
Paris: Two Cities Editions, 1960
The Exterminator (with Brion Gysin), San Francisco: Auerhahn Press, 1960
The Yage Letters (with Allen Ginsberg), San Francisco:
City Lights Books, 1963
Electronic Revolution (with Brion Gysin and Henri Chopin), Massachusetts:
Blackmoor Head Press, 1971
Sidetripping (with Charles Gatewood), New York: Strawberry Hill, 1975
The Third Mind (with Brion Gysin), New York: Viking Press, 1978
The Streets of Chance (with Howard Buchwald), New York:
Red Ozier Press, 1981
The Cat Inside (with Brion Gysin), New York: Grenfell Press, 1986
Apocalypse (with Keith Haring), New York: George Mulder Fine Arts, 1988
The Valley (with Keith Haring), New York: George Mulder Fine Arts, 1989

Comprehensive bibliographies can be found in:

William S. Burroughs: An Annotated Bibliography of His Works and Criticism
by Michael B. Goodman, New York: Garland Publishing, 1975
William S. Burroughs: A Bibliography 1953–1973 by Barry Miles and Joe
Maynard, Charlottesville: University Press of Virginia, 1978
Ports of Entry: William S. Burroughs and the Arts by Robert A. Sobieszek,

London: Thames and Hudson, 1996. (Also contains an exhaustive list of Burroughs art criticism and exhibitions.)

William Burroughs: The Algebra of Need, Eric Mottram, London: Marion Boyars, 1977

William S. Burroughs, Jennie Serkl, Boston: Twayne Publishers, 1987

Word Cultures: Radical Theory and Practice in William S. Burroughs' Fiction,
Robin Lydenberg, Urbana: University of Illinois Press, 1987

Literary Outlaw: The Life and Times of William S. Burroughs,
Ted Morgan, New York: Henry Holt, 1988

William Burroughs: El Hombre Invisible, a Portrait,
Barry Miles, New York: Hyperion, 1993

Discography

Laurie Anderson, *Big Science*, Warner, 1983
The Elvis of Letters (with Gus Van Sant), Tim/Kerr, 1985
Laurie Anderson, *Home of the Brave*, Warner Bros, 1986
Material, Seven Souls, Virgin, 1989
Dead City Radio, Island, 1990
Ministry, *Just One Fix*, Warner, 1992
The Disposable Heroes of Hiphoprisy, *Spare Ass Annie and Other Tales*, Island 1993
Kurt Cobain, *The 'Priest', They Called Him*, Tim/Kerr, 1993
Tom Waits, *The Black Rider*, Island, 1993

Internet

An extensive list of spoken-word recordings can be found at the Burroughs File on the Net.

Index

Page numbers in *italic*
refer to illustrations

A

The Adding Machine
47, 163
Algren, Nelson 77, 80
Anderson, Laurie 193-4
Ansen, Alan 91, 113

B

Balch, Anthony
115-16, 140-1, 183
Ballard, J.G. 217
Beatles *192*, 193
Beiles, Sinclair 93
Betsellie, Melvin 209
Bill and Tony 115
Black, Jack 36
The Black Rider
194, 199-202
Bockris, Victor
29, 137, *138*, 147, 207
Book of Dreams
155, 211
Bowles, Paul 85-9
Brady, John 125
Burroughs, Billy Jnr
71, 75, 116, 119-
21, 141-2, *142*
Burroughs family
25, 28-32, 127

C

Calder, John 99-105
Carr, Lucien 55-9
Cassady, Neal 70, 71
Chappaqua 120
Ciardi, John 99
Cities of the Red Night
131-5, 139, 142
Cobain, Kurt 18, 196,
198-9, *199*
Connell, A.J.
37, 38, 40
Corso, Gregory
75, *76*, 93, 111, 113
Crawdaddy 131
Cronenberg, David
105, 180-7, *182*
The Cut-Ups 115

D

Dead City Radio 195-7
Dead Fingers Talk 101
Dead Roads 152-3
Dent, Dr J. 84, 107
Dillon, Matt *178*, 179
The Disposable Heroes
197-8
Drugstore Cowboy
131, 177-81, *178*

E

Eliot, T.S.
22, *34*, 35, 41
Elvins, Kells *34*, 36,
47-50, 69, 72, 91
Evans, Mary 35
Exterminator!
55, 111, 124, 127

G

Genet, Jean
122, 123, 156
Gibson, W. 139-40
Ginsberg, Allen
22, 57-9, *62*, 63-7, 71,
75, 79-84, 89-99, *98*,
113, *122*, 127-9, 142,
207-9, *212*, 213
Giorno, John
147, *158*, 193
Girodias, Maurice
87, 93-5, 113
Grauerholz, James
129, *130*, *138*, 147, 156,
177, 183, 197
Gysin, Brion
18, 85-9, *96*, 97-9, *108*-
10, 111, 114, 116-
17, 156-7, 173, 183

H

Healy, John 72
Himes, Chester 93
Home of the Brave 194
Huncke, Herbert *60*,
61-3, 67, 69

J

The Job 125
Junkie
27-8, 72, 77-9, *78*

K

Kammerer, David 55-9
Kentucky Ham 29, 116
Kerouac, Jack
17, 22, 59-61, 66-7, 79,
89-91, 123, *124*,
127, 189
Kittredge, G.L. 41
Klapper, Ilse 45-7
Korzybski, Alfred 50

L

Laswell, Bill 194
Leary, Timothy
114, *138*, 213
Lee family 25-8
'Les Voleurs' 197-8
'Letter From a Master
Addict...' 84

M

McCarthy, Mary 99-101
Mailer, Norman
99-101, 123, 155, 169
Masterson, Ray 51
Material 194
Matthiessen, F.O. 41
'Meet Me in
St Louis Louie' 35
Miles, Barry 12, 205
Miller, Bob 45
Minutes to Go 111

N

The Naked Lunch
55, 79, 83-4, *86*-7, 90-
1, 95-105, 181-7,
182, 193
'The Name Is Burroughs'
37, 49
Nirvana 196, 198
Nova Express 107, 111

O

Odier, Daniel 125
Olson, Charles 127
Orlovsky, Peter
90-1, 95, *98*, 113

P

Parker, Edie 59, 66
Port of Saints 124
Portman, M. 113, 115
'The "Priest",
They Called Him' 199

Q

Queer 77, 157-61

R

Rosenthal, Irving 95
Rosset, Barney 95

S

Seven Souls 194-5
Smith, Patti *134*, 135
Sobieszek, R.A. 169
The Soft Machine
101, 111, *114*
Solomon, Carl 75-7
Sommerville, Ian
107, 110, 113-21, 140-1
Southern, Terry
123, 127, 183
Spare Ass Annie 197

T

The Third Mind 117
The Ticket that Exploded
101, 107, 111
Towers Open Fire
53, 115
Trocchi, A. 95, 115
'Twilight's Last
Gleamings' 49-50
Tzara, Tristan 97, *106*

V

Van Sant, Gus 177-9
Vollmer, Joan
63-73, *66*, 201

W

Waits, Tom 199-202
Watson, Alan 119
The Western Lands
153-6, 194-5
The Wild Boys
111, 123-5
Willett, John 101
Williams, Tennessee 156
Willner, Hal 195-7
Wilson, Robert 199
Wylie, Andrew 152
Wyn, A.A. 77

Y

Yage Letters 75, 79

Picture Credits

The author and editors are grateful to the following photographers, photographic agencies, libraries and institutions who provided photographs and visual reference material for this book (listed in alphabetical order followed by page numbers).

AMERICAN ACADAMY OF ARTS AND LETTERS: 20; ARIZONA STATE UNIVERSITY: 110 (Ian Sommerville); CHARLES BABBAGE INSTITUTE: 29, 30, 31, 32; ESTATE OF JEAN-MICHEL BASQUIAT: 168 bottom right; JON BLUMB: 8-9, 17, 52, 166, 167, 186 main picture, 206, 207, 108 bottom, 186 main picture, 206, 207, 208 bottom, 209, 211, 215 bottom; VICTOR BOCKRIS: 136 right inset, 162, 170 bottom, 172 left, 189, 205; UDO BREGER: 195, 219; BRITISH FILM INSTITUTE: 53, 178-179, 180, 181, 182, 184, 187; JOHN BURROUGHS SCHOOL, ST LOUIS: 58 top right; WILLIAM BURROUGHS COMMUNICATIONS: 21; CAMERA PRESS: 16 bottom left, 80 bottom (Sue Adler), 212 bottom; CAROLINE CASSADY: 70; CORBIS: 16 top, bottom right, 62 main picture, 64 main pictures, 65 main pictures, 76 main picture, 80 top right, 90, 91, 98-99, 102-103; *CRAWDADDY*/UNIVERSITY OF CONNECTICUT WILBUR CROSS LIBRARY: 132-133; EMI/PARLOPHONE/MC PRODUCTIONS: 192, 193; ALAN GINSBERG: 45, 66 top left, 60 main picture, 62 top left, bottom, 72, 76 inset, 82 main pictures, 112 main picture; HARVARD UNIVERSITY ARCHIVES: 34 bottom, 35, 42, 43; SIMON JENNINGS ARCHIVE: (graphic ephemera and *objet trouvé*; painted backgrounds and collage by Simon Jennings) 46, 54, 56, 60 insets, 64 background and inset, 65 background and inset, 69, 72, 73, 75, 80 top left, 82 right, 83, 84 inset, 88, 93, 94, 95, 112 background, 119, 120 bottom, 126 right insets, 146-147 background, 151, 152, 153, 154 left, 155; *LIFE MAGAZINE*, TIME, INC.: 122 inset (Perry C. Riddle), 168 top left, top right (Arnold Newman); LOS ALAMOS HISTORICAL MUSEUM: 36, 37 (Laura Gilpin), 38, 39, 40; FRED W. MCDARRAH: 104, 120 right, 122 main picture; *MADEMOISELLE*/CONDE NASTE PUBLICATIONS, INC.: 71, 212 right; G. MALANGA: 108, 109, 116, 126 main picture; MISSOURI HISTORICAL SOCIETY: 34 top; *NEW YORK TIMES*: 58 bottom, 86-87 foreground text, 212 background, 218; PRINCETON UNIVERSITY, SEELEY G. MUDD MANUSCRIPT LIBRARY: 26, 27; RCA RECORDS: 136 background picture (Mick Rock); REDFERNS: 126 bottom left (Caroline Greville Morris), 136 left inset (Ian Dickson), 190 (top row, from left: Erica Echenberg, Ebet Roberts, Leon Morris; middle row, from left: Mick Hudson, Ebet Roberts, Mick Hudson; bottom row, from left: Dave Ellis, Mick Hudson, Chuck Boyd), 196 (Michael Linssen), 199 (Michael Linssen), 200 (Ebet Roberts); MARCIA RESNICK: 96, 138, 143, 144-145, 148-149, 154 right, 203; KATE SIMON: 129, 130, 134, 146 inset, 158-159, 174, 175, 177, 191, 210, 214, 215 top, 216; LAWRENCE L. SMITH: 124; SMITHSONIAN INSTITUTE AND NATIONAL ARCHIVE: 208 top, middle; *TIMES LITERARY SUPPLEMENT*: 100-101; GEORGE UNDERWOOD: 78; JAMES VAN DER ZEE: 168 bottom left. **Note:** The William S. Burroughs silhouette motif which appears throughout the book is inspired by a photograph by JOHN HAYES JNR.

Every effort has been made to contact the owners of copyright photographs included in this volume. Bloomsbury Publishing Plc would appreciate contact from any uncredited copyright holders.